Economics For Business Management

OrangeBooks Publication

1st Floor, Rajhans Arcade, Mall Road, Kohka, Bhilai, Chhattisgarh 490020

Website:**www.orangebooks.in**

© Copyright, 2024, Author

All rights reserved. No part of this book may be reproduced, stored in a retrieval system, or transmitted, in any form by any means, electronic, mechanical, magnetic, optical, chemical, manual, photocopying, recording or otherwise, without the prior written consent of its writer.

First Edition, 2024

ECONOMICS FOR BUSINESS MANAGEMENT

DR. NILA A CHOTAI || DR. MANIKANDAN

OrangeBooks Publication
www.orangebooks.in

INDEX

Chapter 1
Meaning And Importance Of Managerial Economics 1

1.1 Introduction 1
1.2 Meaning 2
1.3 Scope of Managerial Economics 3
1.4 Importance of the Study of Managerial Economics 7
1.5 Two Major Functions of a Managerial Economist 8
1.6 Summary 9
1.7 Terminal Questions 10

Chapter-2
Demand Theory and Concepts 11

2.1 Meaning of Demand 11
2.2 Determinant of Demand 12

Chapter-3
Law of Demand 15

3.1 Market Demand Schedule 17
3.2 Expansion and Contraction of Demand 20
3.3 Increase and Decrease in Demand Curve 21
3.4 Point Elasticity 23
3.5 Demand Distinctions 25
3.6 Questions 26

Chapter-4

Cost 28

4.1 Accounting Costs And Economic Costs 28

4.1 Short Run Average Cost 33

Chapter 5

Production Analysis 39

5.1 Introduction 40

5.2 Meaning of Production Function 40

5.3 Uses Of Production Function 43

5.4 Types Of Production Function 43

5.5 Production Isoquant 45

5.6 Types of Isoquants 45

5.7 Derivation of Smooth Convex Isoquant 48

5.8 Properties Of Isoquants 50

5.9 Isocost 52

5.10 Producers Equilibrium or Optimal Combination of Inputs 53

5.11 Managerial Uses of Production Function 56

5.12 Production Function with One Variable Input Case (Short Run Production Function) 57

5.13 The Law of Variable Proportions (Long Run Production Function) 58

5.14 Economies of Scale 68

5.15 Economies of Scope 77

5.16 Summary 79

5.17 Terminal Questions 80

Chapter 6

Meaning of Market and Market Structure 81

6.1 Introduction 84

Chapter 7

Market Structure 86

7.1 Introduction 87
Exercise: 98
Monopoly Market 99
Review Questions: 104
Degrees Of Price Discrimination: 112

Case Studies 115
Impact Of The Reforms 120
Conclusion 122

Chapter 1

Meaning And Importance Of Managerial Economics

Structure:

1.1 Introduction

1.2 Meaning

1.3 Scope of Managerial Economics

1.4 Importance of the study of Managerial Economics

1.5 Two Major Functions of a Managerial Economist

1.6 Summary

1.7 Questions

1.1 Introduction

Economics touches the lives of all of us. It also takes managers into its folds. Any business is part of an economy. The business must be impacted by the economy and the events happening in the economy. The per capita income of the citizens will define the purchasing power based on which the business enterprises will decide what products to manufacture and sell. A new enterprise has to forecast the demand for the product which it wants to sell. The day to day vegetable market has to decide on a viable price depending upon the interaction between the demand and the supply. Thus management practitioners and academicians brought economics to their perspective and developed, 'Managerial Economics.'

1.2 Meaning

Managerial economics is a science that deals with the application of various economic theories, principles, concepts and techniques to business management in order to solve business and management problems. It deals with the practical application of economic theory and methodology to decision-making problems faced by private, public and non-profit making organizations.

The same idea has been expressed by Spencer and Seigelman in the following words. "Managerial Economics is the integration of economic theory with business practice for the purpose of facilitating decision making and forward planning by the management." According to McNair and Meriam, "Managerial economics is the use of economic modes of thought to analyze business situation". Brighman and Pappas define Managerial economics as," the application of economic theory and methodology to business administration practice." Joel Dean is of the opinion that use of economic analysis in formulating business and management policies is known as managerial economics.

Features of Managerial Economics

It is more realistic, pragmatic and highlights on practical application of various economic theories to solve business and management problems.

It is a science of decision-making. It concentrates on decision-making process, decision models and decision variables and their relationships.

It is both conceptual and metrical and it helps the decision-maker by providing measurement of various economic variables and their interrelationships.

It uses various macroeconomic concepts like national income, inflation, deflation, trade cycles etc to understand and adjust its policies to the environment in which the firm operates.

It also gives importance to the study of non-economic variables having implications of economic performance of the firm. For example, impact of technology, environmental forces, socio-political and cultural factors.

It uses the services of many other sister sciences like mathematics, statistics, engineering, accounting, operation research and psychology etc to find solutions to business and management problems.

It should be clearly remembered that Managerial Economics does not provide ready-made solutions to all kinds of problems faced by a firm. It provides only the logic and methodology to find out answers and not the answers themselves. It all depends on the manager's ability, experience, expertise and intelligence to use different tools of economic analysis to find out the correct answers to business problems.

1.3 Scope of Managerial Economics

The term "scope" indicates the area of study, boundaries, subject matter and width of a subject. Business economics is comparatively a new and upcoming subject. Consequently, there is no unanimity among different economists with respect to the exact scope of business economics. However, the following topics are covered in this subject.

1. Objectives of a Firm

Profit maximization has been considered as the main objective of a business unit in olden days. Today, there are multiple objectives and they are multi dimensional in nature. Some of them are competitive while others are supplementary in nature. A few others are inter-connected and a few others are opposing in nature. There are economic, social, organizational, human, and national goals. All the objectives are determined by various factors and forces like corporate environment, socio-economic conditions, and nature of power in the organization and external constraints under which a firm operates. In the midst of several objectives, the traditional profit maximization objective even today has a very high place. All other policies and programmes of a firm revolve round this objective.

2. Demand Analysis and Forecasting

A firm is basically a producing unit. It produces different kinds of goods and services. It has to meet the requirements of consumers in the market. The basic problems of what to produce, where to produce, for whom to produce, how to produce, how much to produce and how to distribute them in the market are to be answered by a firm. Hence, it has to study in detail the various determinants of demand, nature, composition and characteristics of demand, elasticity of demand, demand distinctions, demand forecasting and so on. The production plan prepared by a firm should take all these points into account.

3. Production and Cost Analysis

Production implies transformation of inputs into outputs. It may be either in physical or monetary terms. The physical production deals with how output is to be produced by a firm by employing different factor inputs in proper proportions. Maximization of output is one of the basic goals of a firm. Production analysis deals with production function, laws of returns, returns to scale, economies of scale, etc. Production cost is concerned with estimation of costs to produce a given quantity of output. Cost controls, cost reduction, cost cutting and cost minimization receive top most priority in production and cost analysis. Maximization of output with minimum cost is the basic slogan of any firm. Cost analysis deals with the study of various cost concepts, their classification, cost-output relationship in the short run and long run.

4. Pricing Decisions, Policies and Practices

Pricing decision is related to fixing the prices of goods and services. This depends on the pricing policy and practices adopted by a firm. Price setting is one of the most important policies of a firm. The amount of revenue, the level of income and above all the volume of profits earned by a firm directly depend on its pricing decisions. Hence, we have to study price-output determination under different market conditions, objectives and considerations of pricing policies, pricing methods, practices, policies etc. we also study price forecasting, marketing channel, distribution channel, sales promotion policies etc.

5. Profit Management

A firm is basically a commercial or business unit. Consequently, the success or failure of it is measured in terms of the amount of profit it is able to earn in a competitive market. The management gives top most priority to this aspect. Under profit management, one has to study various theories of profit, emergence of profit, functions of profit, and its measurement, profit policies, techniques, profit planning, profit forecasting and Break Even Point.

6. Capital Management

It is another crucial area of business. Success of any business depends on adequate capital investment and its proper management. Basically one has to study the cost of employing capital and the rate of return expected from each and every project. It is cost-benefit analysis. Under capital management, one has to study capital requirement, methods of capital mobilization, capital budgeting, optimal allocation of capital, selection of highly profitable projects, cost of capital, return on capital, planning and control of capital expenditure etc.

7. Linear Programming and the Theory of Games

The term linear means that the relationships handled are the same as those represented by straight lines and programming implies systematic planning or decision-making. It implies maximization or minimization of a linear function of variables subject to a constraint of linear inequalities. It offers actual numerical solution to the problems of making optimum choices. It involves either maximization of profits or minimization of costs.

The theory of games basically attempts to explain what is the rational course of action for an individual firm or an entrepreneur who is confronted with the a situation where in the outcome depends not only on his own actions, but also on the actions of others who are also confronted with the same problem of selecting a rational course of action. In short, under the conditions of conflicts and uncertainty, a firm or an individual faces problem similar to that of the player of any game. Both these techniques are extensively used in business economics to solve various business and managerial problems.

8. Market Structure and Conditions

The knowledge of market structure and conditions existing in various kinds of markets are of great importance in any business. The number of sellers and buyers, the nature, extent and degree of competition etc determines the nature of policies to be adopted by a firm in the market.

9. Strategic Planning

It provides a framework on which long term decisions can be made which have an impact on the behavior of the firm. The firm sets certain long-term goals and objectives and selects the strategy to achieve the same. It is now a new addition to the scope of business economics with the emergence of MNCs. The perspective of strategic planning is global. In fact, the integration of business economics and strategic planning has given rise to a new area of study called corporate economics.

10. Other Areas

a. Macroeconomic management of the country relating to economic system, national income, trade cycles Savings and investments and its impact on the working of a firm.

b. Budgetary operations of the government and its implications on the firm.

c. Knowledge and information about various government policies like monetary, fiscal, physical, industrial, labor, foreign trade, foreign capital and technology, MNCs etc and their impact on the working of a firm.

d. Impact of liberalization, globalization, privatization and marketization on the operations of firm.

e. Impact of international changes, role of international financial and trade institutions in formulating domestic polices of a firm.

f. Problems of environmental degradation and pollution and its impact on the policies of a firm.

g. Improvements in the field of science and technology and its impact on a firm etc

h. Socio-political, cultural and other external forces and their influence of business operations.

Thus it is clear that the scope of managerial economics is expanding with the growth of modern business and business environment.

1.4 Importance of the Study of Managerial Economics

Managerial Economics does not give importance to the study of theoretical economic concepts. Its main concern is to apply theories to find solutions to day-to-day practical problems faced by a firm. The following points indicate the significance of the study of this subject in its right perspective.

It gives guidance for identification of key variables in decision-making process.

It helps the business executives to understand the various intricacies of business and managerial problems and to take right decision at the right time.

It provides the necessary conceptual, technical skills, toolbox of analysis and techniques of thinking and other such most modern tools and instruments like elasticity of demand and supply, cost and revenue, income and expenditure, profit and volume of production etc to solve various business problems.

It is both a science and an art. In the context of globalization, privatization, liberalization and mercerization and a highly competitive dynamic economy, it helps in identifying various business and managerial problems, their causes and consequence, and suggests various policies and programs to overcome them.

It helps the business executives to become much more responsive, realistic and competent to face the ever changing challenges in the modern business world.

It helps in the optimum use of scarce resources of a firm to maximize its profits.

It also helps in achieving other objectives a firm like attaining industry leadership, market share expansion and social responsibilities etc.

It helps a firm in forecasting the most important economic variables like demand, supply, cost, revenue, price, sales and profit etc and formulate sound business polices.

It also helps in understanding external factors and forces which affect the decision-making of a firm. Thus, it has become a highly useful and practical discipline in recent years to analyze and find solutions to various kinds of problems in a systematic and rational manner.

1.5 Two Major Functions of a Managerial Economist

A Managerial Economist is a specialist and an expert in analyzing and finding answers to business and managerial problems. He has in-depth knowledge of the subject. He is an authority and has total command over his subject.

A Managerial Economist has to perform several functions in an in an organization. Among them, decision-making and forward planning is described as the two major functions and all other functions are derived from these two basic functions. A detailed description of the two functions is given below for a understanding.

1. Decision-Making

The word "decision" suggests a deliberate choice made out of several possible alternative courses of action after carefully considering them. The act of choice signifying solution to an economic problem is economic decision making. It involves choices among a set of alternative courses of action.

Decision-making is essentially a process of selecting the best out of many alternative opportunities or courses of action that are open to a management.

The choice made by the business executives are difficult, crucial and have far-reaching consequences. The basic aim of taking a decision is to select the best course of action which maximizes the economic benefits and minimizes the use of scarce resources of a firm. Hence, each decision involves cost-benefit analysis. Any slight error or delay in decision making may cause considerable economic and financial damage to a firm. It is for this reason, management experts are of the opinion that right decision – making at the right time is the secret of a successful manager.

2. Forward Planning

The term planning implies a consciously directed activity with certain predetermined goals and means to carry them out. It is a deliberate activity. It is a programmed action. Basically planning is concerned with tackling future situations in a systematic manner.

Forward planning implies planning in advance for the future. It is associated with deciding the future course of action of a firm. It is prepared on the basis of past and current experience of a firm. It is prepared in the background of uncertain and unpredictable environment and guess work. Future events and happenings cannot be predicted accurately. Growing firms devote a significant share of their current output to net capital formation to bolster future economic output. A business executive must be sufficiently intelligent enough to think in advance, prepare a sound plan and take all possible precautionary measures to meet all types of challenges of the future business. Hence, forward planning has acquired greater significance in business circles.

1.6 Summary

Managerial economics is a new and a highly specialized branch of economics. It brings together economic theory and business practice. It assists in applying various economic theories and principles to find solutions to business and management problems.

It is applied economics and makes an attempt to explain how various economic concepts are usefully employed in business management. It is a practical subject. It opens up the mind of a managerial economist to the complex and highly challenging business world. The features of managerial economics throw light on the nature of the emerging subject and the scope gives information about the wide coverage of the subject. The concepts of decision-making and forward planning are the two basic functions of a managerial economist. In a way the entire subject matter of managerial economics is to be understood in the background of these two functions.

1.7 Terminal Questions

1. Define Managerial Economics and explain its main characteristics.
2. Discuss the scope of Managerial Economics.
3. Explain the importance of Managerial Economics.
4. Discuss the functions of a Managerial Economist.
5. "Managerial economics is an integration of economic theory, decision science and business management" Comment.

Chapter-2

Demand Theory and Concepts

Structure:

2.1 Meaning of Demand

2.2 Determinant of Demand

2.1 Meaning of Demand

The concept 'demand' refers to the quantity of a good or service that consumers are willing and able to purchase at various prices during a period of time. It is to be noted that demand in Economics is something more than desire to purchase though desire is one element of it. A beggar, for instance, may desire food, but due to lack of means to purchase it, his demand is not effective. Thus effective demand for a thing depends on (i) desire (ii) means to purchase and (iii) on willingness to use those means for that purchase. Unless demand is backed by purchasing power or ability to pay, it does not constitute demand. Two things are to be noted about quantity demanded. One is that quantity demanded is always expressed at a givenprice. At different prices different quantities of a commodity are generally demanded. The second thing is that quantity demanded is a flow. We are concerned not with a single isolated purchase, but with a continuous flow of purchases and we must therefore express demand as so much per period of time – one thousand dozens oranges per day, seven thousand dozen oranges per week and so on.

In short "By demand, we mean the various quantities of a given commodity or service which consumers would buy in one market in a given period of time, at various prices, or at various incomes, or at various prices of related goods."

2.2 Determinant of Demand

There are a number of factors which influence household demand for a commodity. Important among these are :

i) *Price of the commodity* Ceteris paribus i.e. other things being equal, the demand of acommodity is inversely related to its price. It implies that a rise in price of a commodity brings about a fall in its purchase and vice-versa. This happens because of income and substitution effects.

ii) *Price of related commodities* : Related commodities are of two types : (a) complementary goods and (b) competing goods or substitutes. Complementary goods are those goods which are consumed together or simultaneously. For example, tea and sugar, automobiles and petrol, pen and ink are used together. When commodities are complements, a fall in the price of one (other things being equal) will cause the demand of the other to rise. For example, a fall in the price of cars would lead to a rise in the demand for petrol. Similarly, a fall in the price of pens, will cause a rise in the demand for ink. The reverse will be the case when the price of a complement rises. Competing goods or substitutes are those goods which can be used with ease in place of one another. For example, tea and coffee, ink pen and ball pen, are substitutes for each other and can be used in place of, one another easily. When goods are substitutes, a fall in the price of one (*ceteris paribus*) leads to a fall in the quantity demanded of its substitutes. For example, if the price of tea falls, people will try to substitute it for coffee and demand more of it and less of coffee i.e. the demand for tea will rise and that of coffee fall.

iii) *Level of income of the household* : Other things being equal, the demand for a commodity depends upon the money income of the household. In most cases, the larger the average money income of the household, the larger is the quantity demanded of a particular good. However, there are certain commodities for which quantities demanded decrease with an increase in money income. These goods are called inferior goods. Even in the case of other goods, the response of quantities demanded to changes in their prices is not of same proportions. If goods are such that they satisfy the basic necessities (food, clothing, shelter) of life, a change in their prices although will cause an increase in demand for these necessities this increase will be less than proportionate to the increase in income. This isbecause as people become richer, there is a relative decline in importance of food and other non durable goods in the over all consumption pattern and a rise in importance of durable goods such as a TV, car, house etc.

iv) *Tastes and preferences of consumers* : The demand for a commodity also depends upon tastes and preferences of consumers and changes in them over a period of time. Goods which are more in fashion command higher demand than goods which are out of fashion. Consumers may even discard a good even before it is fully utilised and prefer another good which is in fashion. For example, there is a greater demand for coloured television and more and more people are discarding their black and white television even though they could have still used it for some more years. 'Demonstration effect' plays an important role in affecting the demand for a product. An individual's demand for colour television may be affected by his seeing one in neighbour's or friend's house, either because he likes what he sees or because he figures out that if his neighbour or friend can afford it, he too can. A person may develop a taste or preference for wine after tasting some, but he may also develop it after discovering that serving it enhances his prestige. In any case, people have tastes and preferences and these changes, sometimes due to external and sometimes due to internal causes.

v) *Other factors* : Apart from the above factors, the demand for a commodity depends upon the following factors :

   a) **Size of population** : Generally, larger the size of population of a country or a region, greater is the demand for commodities in general.

   b) **Composition of population** : If there are more old people in a region, the demand for spectacles, walking sticks, etc. will be high. Similarly, if the population consists of more of children, demand for toys, baby foods, toffees, will be more.

c) **Distribution of income** : The wealth of a country may be so distributed that there are a few very rich people while the majority are very poor. Under such conditions the propensity to consume of the country will be relatively less, for the propensity to consume of the rich people is less than that of the poor people. Consequently, the demand for consumer goods will be comparatively less.

Chapter-3

Law of Demand

Structure:

3.1 Market Demand Schedule

3.2 Expansion and Contraction of Demand

3.3 Increase and Decrease in Demand Curve

3.4 Point Elasticity

3.5 Demand Distinctions

3.6 Questions

The law of demand is one of the most important laws of economic theory. According to law of demand, other things being equal, if the price of a commodity falls, the quantity demanded of it will rise and if the price of a commodity rises, its quantity demanded will decline. Thus, there is an inverse relationship between price and quantity demanded, other things being same. The other things which are assumed to be equal or constant are the prices of related commodities, income of consumers, tastes and preferences of consumers, and such other factors which influence demand. If these factors which determine demand also undergo a change, then the inverse price-demand relationship may not hold good. For example, if incomes of consumers increase, then an increase in the price of a commodity, may not result in a decrease in the quantity demanded of it. Thus the constancy of these other factors is an important assumption of the law of demand.

The law of demand may be illustrated with the help of a demand schedule and a demand curve.

1.2.0 Demand Schedule: To illustrate the relation between the quantity of a commodity demanded and its price, we may take hypothetical data for prices and quantities of a commodity X.

Table 1: Demand schedule of an individual consumer

Price	Quantity Demand
30	5
25	10
20	15
15	20
10	25
5	30

From the above table, When price of commodity X is Rs. 30 per unit, a consumer purchases 5 units of the commodity. When the price falls to Rs. 25, he purchases 10 units of the commodity. Similarly, when the price further falls, quantity demanded by him goes on rising until at price Re. 5, the quantity demanded by him rises to 30 units. The above table depicts an inverse relationship between price and quantity demanded as the price of the commodity X goes on rising, its demand goes on falling.

Demand curve: We can now plot the data from Table 1 on a graph with price on the vertical axis and quantity on the horizontal axis.

We now draw a smooth curve through these points. The curve is called the demand curve for commodity 'X'. The curve shows the quantity of 'X' that a consumer would like to buy at a each price; its downward slope indicates that the quantity of 'X' demanded increases as its price falls. Thus the downward sloping demand curve is in accordance with the law of demand which as stated above, describes an inverse price-demand relationship.

3.1 Market Demand Schedule

When we add up the various quantities demanded by the number of consumers in the market we can obtain the market demand schedule. How the summation is done is illustrated in Table 2. Suppose there are three individual buyers of the goods in the market. The Table 2 shows their individual demands at various prices.

Price of Commodity 'X' (in Rs.)

10	20
15	30
20	40
35	65

Table: 2

Market Demand Schedule

Demand of A   Demand of B   Market Demand

(Units)

    5 30

    4 45

    3 60

          2 100

1 62 82 144

From the above table, It is clearly indicates that there are two individual buyers of the goods in the market. When we add quantities demanded at each price by consumers A and B we get total market demand.

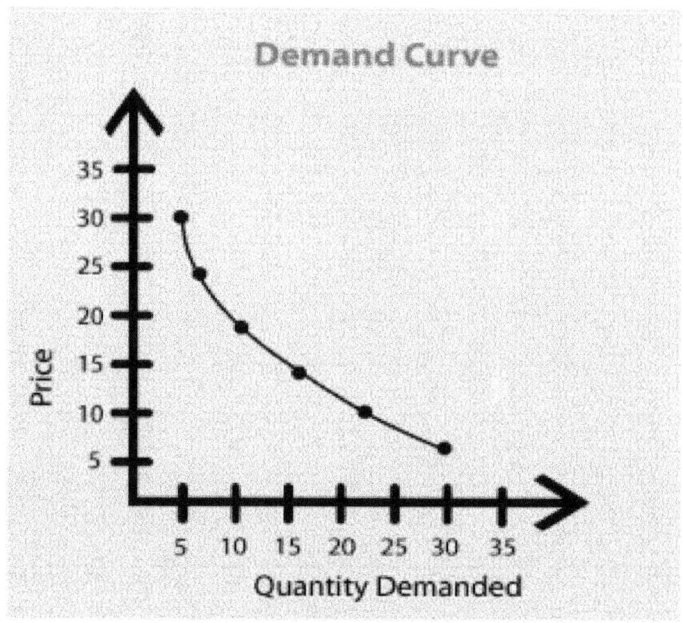

Fig.2

Market Demand Curve

Exceptions of Law of Demand: According to the law of demand, more of commodity will be demanded at lower prices than at higher prices, other things being equal. The law of demand is valid in most of the cases; however there are certain cases where this law does not hold good. The following are the important exceptions to the law of demand.

Conspicuous goods: Articles of prestige value or snob appeal or articles of conspicuous consumption are demanded only by the rich people and these articles become more attractive if their prices go up. Such articles will not conform to the usual law of demand. This was found out by Veblen in his doctrine of "Conspicuous Consumption" and hence this effect is called Veblen effect or prestige goods effect. Veblen effect takes place as some consumers measure the utility of a commodity by its price i.e., if the commodity is expensive they think that it has got more utility. As such, they buy less of this commodity at low price and more of it at high price. Diamonds are often given as example of this case. Higher the price of diamonds, higher is the prestige value attached to them and hence higher is the demand for them.

Giffen goods: Sir Robert Giffen, an economist, was surprised to find out that as the price of bread increased, the British workers purchased more bread and not less of it. This was something against the law of demand. Why did this happen? The reason given for this is that when the price of bread went up, it caused such a large decline in the purchasing power of the poor people that they were forced to cut down the consumption of meat and other more expensive foods. Since bread even when its price was higher than before was still the cheapest food article, people consumed more of it and not less when its price went up. Such goods which exhibit direct price-demand relationship are called 'Giffen goods'. Generally those goods which are considered inferior by the consumers and which occupy a substantial place in consumer's budget are called 'Giffen goods'. Examples of such goods are coarse grains like bajra, low quality of rice and wheat etc.

Conspicuous necessities: The demand for certain goods is affected by the demonstration effect of the consumption pattern of a social group to which an individual belongs. These goods, due to their constant usage, have become necessities of life. For example, in spite of the fact that the prices of television sets, refrigerators, coolers, cooking gas etc. have been continuously rising, their demand does not show any tendency to fall.

Future expectations about prices: It has been observed that when the prices are rising, households expecting that the prices in the future will be still higher, tend to buy larger quantities of the commodities. For example, when there is wide-spread drought, people expect that prices of food grains would rise in future. They demand greater quantities of food grains as their price rise. But it is to be noted that here it is not the law of demand which is invalidated but there is a change in one of the factors which was held constant while deriving the law of demand, namely change in the price expectations of the people.

Demand for Necessaries: The law of demand does not apply much in the case of necessaries of life. Irrespective of price changes, people have to consume the minimum quantities of necessary commodities. Similarly, in practice, a household may demand larger quantity of a commodity even at a higher price because it may be ignorant of the ruling price of the commodity. Under such circumstances, the law will not remain valid.

3.2 Expansion and Contraction of Demand

The demand schedule, demand curve and the law of demand all show that when the price of a commodity falls its quantity demanded increases, other things being equal. When as a result of decrease in price, the quantity demanded increases, in Economics, we say that there is an expansion of demand and when as a result of increase in price, quantity demanded decreases we say that there is contraction of demand. For example, suppose the price of apples at any time is Rs. 20 per kilogram and a consumer buys 1 kilogram at that price. Now, if other things such as income, prices of other goods and tastes of the consumers remain same but the price of apples falls to Rs. 15 per kilogram and the consumer now buys 2 kilograms of apples, we say that there is a change in quantity demanded or there is an expansion of demand. On the contrary, if the price of apples rises to Rs. 25 per kilogram and consumer buys only half a kilogram, we say that there is a contraction of demand.

The phenomena of expansion and contraction in demand are shown in Figure 3. The figure shows that when price is OP quantity demanded is OM, given other things equal. If as a result of increase in price (OP"), the quantity demanded falls to OL we say there is 'a fall in quantity demanded' or 'contraction of demand' or 'an upward movement along the same curve'. Similarly, as a result of fall in price to OP' the quantity demanded rises to ON, we say that there is 'expansion of demand' or 'a rise in quantity demanded' or 'a downward movement on the same demand curve.'

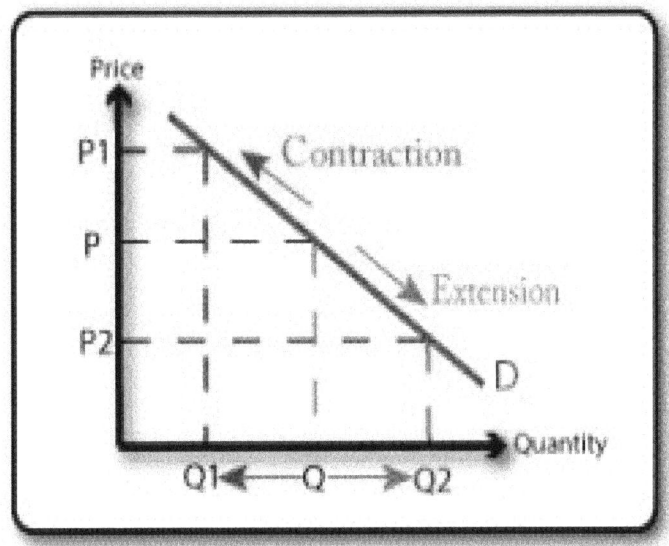

Fig: 3

Extension and Contraction of Demand curve

Till now we have assumed that other determinants remain constant when we are analyzing demand for a commodity. It should be noted that expansion and contraction in demand take place as a result of changes in the price while all other determinants of price viz. income, tastes, propensity to consume and price of related goods remain constant. These other factors remaining constant means that the position of the demand curve remains the same and the consumer moves downwards or upwards on it. What happens if there is a change in, Consumers' tastes and preferences, income, the prices of the related goods or other factors on which demand depends?

3.3 Increase and Decrease in Demand Curve

A rightward shift in the demand curve: (when more is demanded at each price) can be caused by a rise in income, a rise in the price of a substitute, a fall in the price of a complement, a change in tastes in favour of this commodity, an increase in population, and a redistribution of income to groups who favor this commodity.

A leftward shift in the demand curve: (when less is demanded at each price) can be caused by a fall in income, a fall in the price of a substitute, a rise in the price of a complement, a change in tastes against this commodity, a decrease in population, and a redistribution of income away from groups who favour this commodity.

Elasticity of Demand

Elasticity of demand is defined as the responsiveness of the quantity demanded of a good to changes in one of the variables on which demand depends or we can say that it is the percentage change in quantity demanded divided by the percentage in one of the variables on which demand depends. These variables are price of the commodity, prices of the related commodities, income of the consumers and other various factors on which demand depends. Thus we have price elasticity, cross elasticity, elasticity of substitution and income elasticity. It is to be noted that when we talk of elasticity of demand, unless and until otherwise mentioned, we talk of price elasticity of demand. In other words, it is price elasticity of demand which is usually referred to as elasticity of demand.

Price Elasticity: Price elasticity of demand expresses the response of quantity demanded of a good to a change in its price, given the consumer's income, his tastes and prices of all other goods. In other words, it is measured as percentage change in quantity demanded divided by the percentage change in price, other things remaining equal.

Problems

The price of a commodity decreases from Rs.8 to Rs.6 and quantity demanded for good increases from 10 units to 15 units. Find the coefficient of price elasticity.

Solution: Price elasticity = $(-) dq/dp \times p/q = 5/2 \times 8/10 = (-) 2$

Types of Price Elasticity of Demand

Elasticity is zero, if there is no change at all in quantity demanded when price changes i.e. when quantity demanded does not respond to a price change. Elasticity is one, or unitary, if the percentage change in quantity demanded is equal to the percentage change in price.

Elasticity is greater than one when the percentage change in quantity demanded is greater than the percentage change in price. In such a case, demand is said to be elastic. Elasticity is less than one when the percentage change in quantity demanded is less than the percentage change in price. In such a case demand is said to be inelastic.

Elasticity is infinite, when some 'small price reduction raises the demand from zero to infinity. Under such a case consumers will buy all that they can obtain of the commodity at some price. If there is a slight increase in price, they would not buy anything from the particular seller. This type of demand curve is found in perfectly competitive market.

3.4 Point Elasticity

In point elasticity, we measure elasticity at a given point on a demand curve. Point elasticity makes use of derivative rather than finite changes in price and quantity. It is to be noted that elasticity is different at different points on the same demand curve. Given a straight line demand curve tT, point elasticity at any point say R can be found by using formula.

Point Elasticity of Demand

Total Outlay Method of Calculating Price Elasticity

The price elasticity of demand for a commodity and the total expenditure or outlay made on it is greatly related to each other. By analyzing the changes in total expenditure or outlay we can know the price elasticity of demand for the good. However, it should be noted that by this method we can only say whether a good is elastic or inelastic; we cannot find out the exact coefficient of $q q p p$ Elasticity = q q p p elasticity.

Arc Elasticity of Demand

$$\varrho = p\ q\ dq\ dp$$

When the price change is somewhat larger or when price elasticity is to be found between the two prices [or two points on the demand curve say A and B], the question arise which price and quantity should be taken as base. This is because elasticity's found by using original price and quantity will be different from the one derived by using new price and quantity figures.

Arc Elasticity of Demand

Income Elasticity of Demand: Income elasticity of demand is the degree of responsiveness of quantity demanded of a goods to a small change in the income of consumers. In symbolic form,

$$\frac{\text{Percentage change in quantity demanded}}{\text{Percentage change on income}}$$

Cross Elasticity of Demand

The demand for a particular commodity may change due to the changes of prices of related goods. These related goods may be either complementary goods or substitute goods. This type of relationship is studied under 'Cross Demand'. Cross demand refers to the quantities of a commodity or service which will be purchased with reference to changes, not of that particular commodity, but of other inter-related commodities, other things remaining the same. It may be defined as the quantities of a commodity that consumers buy per unit of time at different prices of a 'related article'. 'Other things remaining the same' is the assumption which means that the income of the consumer and also the price of the commodity in question will remain constant.

In the substitute commodities the cross demand curve slopes upwards (i.e. is positive) showing that more quantities of a commodity will be demanded whenever there is a rise in price of a substitute commodity. In the case of complementary goods, a change in price of a good will has an opposite reaction on the demand of other commodity which is closely related or complementary. A change in the demand for one goods in response to a change in the price of another goods represents cross elasticity of demand of the former goods for the latter goods.

$$Ec = qx/py \times py/qx$$

Where Ec stands for cross elasticity.

- qx stands for original quantity demanded of X.

- Δqx stands for change in quantity demanded of X
- py stands for the original price of good Y.
- Δpy stands for a small change in the price of Y.

If two goods are perfect substitutes for each other cross elasticity is infinite and if two goods are totally unrelated, cross elasticity between them is zero.

3.5 Demand Distinctions

The demand distinctions are

a. Producers goods and Consumer's goods.

b. Durable goods and Non-durable goods.

c. Derived demand and Autonomous demand.

d. Industry demand and Company demand.

e. Short-run demand and Long-run demand.

Producer's goods and Consumer's goods:

Producer's goods are those which are used for the production of other goods- either consumer goods or producer goods themselves. Examples of such goods are machines, locomotives, ships etc. Consumer's goods are those which are used for final consumption. Examples of consumer's goods can be readymade clothes, prepared food, residential houses, etc.

Durable goods and Non-durable goods:

Consumer's goods may be further sub-divided into durable and non-durable goods. The non durable consumer goods are those which cannot be consumed more than once; for example bread, milk etc. These will meet only the current demand. On the other hand, durable consumer goods are those which can be consumed more than once over a period of time, example, a car, a refrigerator, a ready-made shirt, and umbrella. The demand for durable goods is likely to be a derived demand.

Derived demand and Autonomous demand

When a product is demanded consequent on the purchase, of a parent product, its demand is called derived demand. For example, the demand for cement is derived demand, being directly related to building activity. If the demand for a product is independent of demand for other goods, then it is called autonomous demand. But this distinction is purely arbitrary and it is very difficult to find out which product is entirely independent of other products.

Industry demand and Company demand

The term industry demand is used to denote the total demand for the products of a particular industry, e.g. the total demand for steel in the country. On the other hand, the term company demand denotes the demand for the products of a particular company, e.g. demand for steel produced by the Tata Iron and Steel Company.

Short –run demand and Long-run demand

Short run demand refers to demand with its immediate reaction to price changes, income fluctuations, etc., whereas long-run demand is that which will ultimately exists as a result of the changes in pricing, promotion or product improvement, after enough time is allowed to let the market adjust to the new situation. For example, if electricity rates are reduced, in the short run, the existing users will make greater use of electric appliances. In the long run more and more people will be induced to use electric appliances.

3.6 Questions

1. What is demand?
2. What are the factors influencing Demand?
3. What are the exceptions of Law of Demand?
4. Differentiate Extension and Contraction and Increase and Decrease in Demand Curve.
5. Define Elasticity of demand.
6. What is price elasticity of demand?

7. Explain the various types of price elasticity of demand.
8. What is income elasticity of demand?
9. Explain cross Elasticity of demand.
10. Briefly explain the Demand Distinction.

✦ ◆ ✦

Chapter-4

Cost

Structure:

4.1 Accounting Costs And Economic Costs.

4.2 Short Run Average Cost.

Cost analysis refers to the study of behavior of cost in relation to one or more production criteria, namely, size of output, scale of operations, prices of factors of production and other relevant economic variables. In other words, cost analysis is concerned with financial aspects of production relations as against physical aspects which were considered in production analysis. In order to have a clear understanding of the cost function it is important to understand various concepts of costs.

4.1 Accounting Costs And Economic Costs

When an entrepreneur undertakes an act of production he has to pay prices for the factors which he employs for production. He thus pays, wages to workers employed, prices for the raw materials, fuel and power used, rent for the building he hires, and interest on the money borrowed for doing business. All these are included in his cost of production and are termed as accounting costs. Thus accounting costs take care of all the payments and charges made by the entrepreneur to the suppliers of various productive factors. But it generally happens that an entrepreneur invests a certain amount of capital in his business. If the capital invested by the entrepreneur in his business had been invested elsewhere it would have earned certain amount of interest or dividend. Moreover, an entrepreneur devotes time to his own work of production and contributes his entrepreneurial and managerial ability to do business. Had he not set up his own business he would have sold his services to others for some positive amount of money. Accounting costs do not include these costs. These costs form a part of the economic cost. Thus economic costs include:

(1) the normal return on money capital invested by the entrepreneur himself in his own business; (2) the wages or salary not paid to the entrepreneur but could have been earned if the services had been sold somewhere else. Likewise the monetary reward for all factors owned by the entrepreneur himself and employed by him in his own business is also considered a part of economic costs. Thus, accounting costs relate to those costs only which involve cash payments by the entrepreneur of the firm. Economic costs take into account these accounting costs but in addition, they also takes into account the amount of money the entrepreneur could have earned if he had invested his money and sold his own services and other factors in the next best alternative uses.

Accounting costs are also called explicit costs whereas the cost of factors owned by the entrepreneur himself and employed in his own business is called implicit costs. Thus economic costs include both accounting costs and implicit costs. The concept of economic cost is important because an entrepreneur must cover his economic cost if he wants to earn normal profits and abnormal profits are over and above these normal profits. In other words, an entrepreneur is said to be earning profits (abnormal) only when his revenues are able to cover not only his explicit costs but also implicit costs.

Outlay costs and opportunity costs: Outlay costs involve actual expenditure of funds on, say, wages, material, rent, interest, etc. Opportunity cost, on the other hand, is concerned with the cost of foregone opportunity; it involves a comparison between the policy that was chosen and the policy that was rejected. For example, opportunity cost of using capital is the interest that it can earn in the next best use of equal risk. A distinction between outlay costs and opportunity costs can be drawn on the basis of the nature of the sacrifice.

Outlay costs involve financial expenditure at some time and hence are recorded in the books of account. Opportunity costs relate to sacrificed alternatives; they are not recorded in the books of account in general.

The opportunity cost concept is generally very useful, e.g., in a cloth mill which spins its own yarn, the opportunity cost of yarn to the weaving department is the price at which the yarn could be sold, for measuring profitability of the weaving operations. In long-term cost calculation also it is useful e.g., in calculating the cost of higher education, it is not the tuition fee and books but the earning foregone that should be taken into account.

Direct or traceable costs and indirect or non-traceable costs; Direct costs are costs that are readily identified and are traceable to a particular product, operation or plant. Even overhead can be direct as to a department; manufacturing costs can be direct to a product line, sales territory, customer class etc. We must know the purpose of cost calculation before considering whether a cost is direct or indirect.

Indirect costs are not readily identified nor visibly traceable to specific goods, services, operations, etc. but are nevertheless charged to the jobs or products in standard accounting practice. The economic importance of these costs is that these, even though not directly traceable to the product, may bear some functional relationship to production and may vary with output in some definite way. Examples of such costs are electric power, the common costs incurred for general operation of business benefiting all products jointly.

Fixed and variable costs: Fixed or constant costs are not a function of output; they do not vary with output upto a certain level of activity. These costs require a fixed expenditure of funds irrespective of the level of output, e.g., rent, property taxes, interest on loans, depreciation when taken as a function of time and not of output. However, these costs also vary with the size of the plant and are a function of capacity. Therefore, fixed costs do not vary with the volume of output within a capacity level.

Fixed costs cannot be avoided. These costs are fixed so long as operations are going on. They can be avoided only when operations are completely closed down. We can call them as inescapable or uncontrollable costs. But there are some costs which will continue even after operations are suspended, as for example, the storing of old machines which cannot be sold in the market. Some of the fixed costs such as advertising, etc. are programmed fixed costs discretionary expenses, because they do discretionary expenses, because they depend upon the discretion of management whether to spend on these services or not.

Variable costs are costs that are a function of output in the production period. For example, wages and cost of raw materials are variable costs. Variable costs vary directly and sometimes proportionately with output. Over certain ranges of production they may vary less or more than proportionately depending on the utilization of fixed facilities and resources during production process. The cost function refers to the mathematical relation between cost of a product and the various determinants of costs. In cost function, the dependent variable is unit cost or total cost and the independent variables are the price of a factor, the size of the output or any other relevant phenomenon which has a bearing on cost such as technology, level of capacity utilization, efficiency and time period under consideration.

Total, fixed and variable costs: There are some factors which can be easily adjusted with changes in the level of output. Thus a firm can readily employ more workers if it has to increase output. Similarly, it can purchase more raw materials if it has to expand production. Such factors which can be easily varied with a change in the level of output are called variable factors. On the other hand, there are factors such as building, capital equipment, or top management team which cannot be so easily varied. It requires comparatively longer time to make changes in them. It takes time to install new machinery. Similarly, it takes time to build a new factory. Such factors which cannot be readily varied and require a longer period to adjust are called fixed factors. Corresponding to the distinction between variable and fixed factors we distinguish between short run and long run periods of time. Short run is a period of time in which output can be increased or decreased by changing only the amount of variable factors, such as labour, raw material, etc. In the short run, quantities of fixed factors cannot be varied in accordance with changes in output. If the firm wants to increase output in the short run, it can do so only with the help of variable factors, i.e., by using more labour and/or by buying more raw materials. Thus, short run is a period of time in which only variable factors can be varied, while the quantities of fixed factors remain unaltered. On the other hand, long run is a period of time in which the quantities of all factors may be varied. Thus all factors become variable in the long run.

Thus we find that fixed costs are those costs which are independent of output, i.e., they do not change with changes in output. These costs are a "fixed amount" which are incurred by a firm in the short run, whether the output is small or large. Even if the firm closes down for some time in the short run but remains in business, these costs have to be borne by it. Fixed costs include such charges as contractual rent, insurance fee, maintenance cost, property taxes, interest on capital employed, manager's salary, watchman's wages etc. Variable costs on the other hand are those costs which change with changes in output. These costs include payments such as wages of labour employed, prices of raw material, fuel and power used, transportation cost etc. If a firm shuts down for a short period, then it may not use variable factors of production and will not therefore incur any variable cost.

There are some costs which are neither perfectly variable, nor absolutely fixed in relation to the changes in the size of output. They are known as semi-variable costs. **Example:** Electricity charges include both a fixed charge and a charge based on consumption. There are some costs which may increase in a stair-step fashion, i.e., they remain fixed over certain range of output; but suddenly jump to a new higher level when output goes beyond a given limit. Eg. Fixed salary of Foreman will have a sudden jump if another foreman is appointed when the output crosses a limit.

Total cost of a business is thus the sum of total variable cost and total fixed cost or symbolically

$$TC = TFC + TVC.$$

4.1 Short Run Average Cost

Average fixed cost (AFC): AFC is the total fixed cost divided by the number of units of output produced. i.e. Where Q is the number of units produced. Thus average fixed cost is the fixed cost per unit of output. For example, a firm is producing with total fixed cost at Rs. 4,000/-. When output is 100 units, average fixed cost will be Rs. 40. And now if the output increases to 200 units, average fixed cost will be Rs. 20. Since total fixed cost is a constant amount, average fixed cost will steadily fall as output increases.

Average Variable Cost: Average variable cost is the total variable cost divided by number of units of output produced. Thus average variable cost is variable cost per unit of output. Average variable cost normally falls as output increases from zero to normal capacity output due to occurrence of increasing returns. But beyond the normal capacity output, average variable cost will rise steeply because of the operation of diminishing returns (the concepts of increasing returns and diminishing returns have already been discussed earlier).

Average total cost (ATC): Average total cost is a sum of average variable cost and average fixed cost. i.e., ATC = AFC + AVC. It is the total cost divided by the number of units produced. The behaviour of average total cost curve depends upon the behaviour of average variable cost curve and average fixed cost curve. In the beginning both AVC and AFC curves fall, therefore, the ATC curve will also fall sharply in the beginning. When AVC curve begins to rise, but AFC curve still falls steeply, ATC curve continues to fall. This is because during this stage the fall in AFC curve is greater than the rise in the AVC curve but as output increases further, there is a sharp rise in AVC which more than offsets the fall in AFC. Therefore, ATC curve first falls, reaches its minimum and then rises. Thus, the average total cost curve is "U" shape curve.

Marginal Cost: Marginal cost is the addition made to the total cost by production of an additional unit of output. In other words, it is the total cost of producing t units instead of t-1 units, where t is any given number. For example, if we are producing 10 units at a cost of Rs. 200 and now suppose 11th unit is produced and the total cost is Rs. 250, marginal cost is Rs. 250 -

200 i.e., Rs. 50. It is to be noted that marginal cost is independent of fixed cost. This is because fixed costs do not change with output. It is only the variable costs which change with a change in the level of output in the short run. Therefore, marginal cost is in fact due to the changes in variable costs. Symbolically marginal cost can be written as:

$$MC_n = TC_n - TC_{n-1}$$

Marginal cost curve falls as output increases in the beginning. It starts rising after a certain level of output. This happens because of the influence of the law of variable proportions. The fact that marginal product rises first, reaches a maximum and then declines ensures that the marginal cost curve of a firm declines first, reaches its minimum and then rises. In other words Marginal cost curve of a firm is "U" shaped.

Table: 3

A Firm's Short-Run Costs ($)

Rate of output	Fixed cost FC	Variable cost VC	Total cost TC	Marginal cost MC	Average fixed cost AFC	Average variable cost AVC	Average total cost ATC
0	50	0	50				
1	50	50	100	50	50	50	100
2	50	78	128	28	25	39	64
3	50	98	148	20	16.5	32.7	49.3
4	50	112	162	14	12.5	28	40.5
5	50	130	180	18	10	26	36
6	50	150	200	20	8.3	25	33.3
7	50	175	225	25	7.1	25	32.1
8	50	204	254	29	6.3	25.5	31.8
9	50	242	292	38	5.6	26.9	32.4
10	50	300	350	58	5	30	35
11	50	385	435	85	4.5	35	39.5

Short Run Cost Curve

The above table shows that fixed cost does not change with increase in output upto a given range. Average fixed cost, therefore, comes down with every increase in output. Variable cost increases but not necessarily in the same proportion as the increase in output. In the above case, average variable cost comes down gradually till 55 units are produced. Marginal cost is the additional cost divided by addition units produced. This also comes gradually till 44 units are produced.

Relationship between Average Cost and Marginal Cost: The relationship between marginal cost and average cost is the same as that between any other marginal average quantities. The following are the points of relationship between the two phenomena. When average cost falls as a result of an increase in output, marginal cost is less than average cost. When average cost rises as a result of an increase in output, marginal cost is more than average cost. When average cost is minimum, marginal cost is equal to the average cost. In other words, marginal cost curve cuts average cost curve at its minimum point (i.e. optimum point).

Long-run Average Cost Curve

As stated above long run is a period of time during which the firm can vary all of its inputs - unlike short run in which some inputs are fixed and others are variable. In other words, whereas in the short run the firm is tied with a given plant, in the long run the firm moves from one plant to another; it can acquire a big plant if it wants to increase its output and a small plant if it wants to reduce its output. Long run cost of production is the least possible cost of producing any given level of output when all individual factors are variable. A long run cost curve depicts the functional relationship between output and the long run cost of production. In order to understand how long run average cost curve is derived we consider three short run average cost curves as shown in These short run cost curves (SACs) are also called plant curves. In the short run the firm can be operating on any short run average cost curve given the size of the plant. Suppose that these are the only three plants which are technically possible. Given the size of the plant, the firm will be increasing or decreasing its output by changing the amount of the variable inputs. But in the long run, the firm chooses among the three possible sizes of plants as depicted by short run average curve (SAC1, SAC2, SAC3).

In the long run, the firm will examine with which size of plants or on which short average cost curve it should operate to produce a given level of output so that total cost is minimum. It will be seen from the diagram that upto OB amount of output the firm will operate on the SAC1, though it could also produce with SAC2, because upto OB amount of output, the production on SAC1 results in lower cost than on SAC2. For example, if the level of output OA is produced with SAC1, it will cost AL per unit and if it is produced with SAC2 it will cost AH and we can see that AH is more than AL. Similarly, if the firm plans to produce an output which is larger than OB but less than OD then it will not be economical to produce on SAC1. For this, the firm will have to use SAC2. Similarly, the firm will use SAC3 for output larger than OD. It is thus clear that in the long run the firm has a choice in the employment of plant and it will employ that plant which yields minimum possible unit cost for producing a given output.

Suppose now, the firm has a choice so that a plant can be varied by infinitely small gradations so that there are infinite number of plants corresponding to which there numerous average cost curves. In such a case the long run average cost curve will be a smooth curve enveloping all these short run average cost curves. As shown in the long run average cost curve is so drawn as to be tangent to each of the short run average cost curves. Every point on the long run average cost curve will be a tangency point with some short run AC curve. If a firm desires to produce any particular output it then builds a corresponding plant and operate on the corresponding short run average cost curve. As for producing OM the corresponding point on the LAC curve is G and the short run average cost curve SAC2 is tangent to the long run AC at this point. Thus if a firm desires to produce output OM, the firm will construct a plant corresponding to SAC2 and will operate on this curve at point G. Similarly, the firm will produce other levels of output choosing the plant which suits its requirements of lowest possible cost of production.

It is clear from the figure that the large output can be produced at the lowest cost with the larger plant whereas smaller output can be produced at the lowest cost with smaller plants. For example, to produce OM, the firm will be using

SAC2 only; if it uses SAC3 for this, it will result in higher unit cost than SAC2. But larger output OV can be produced most economically with a larger plant represented by the SAC3. If we produce OV with the smaller plant it will result in higher unit similarly if we produce larger output with a smaller plant it will involve higher cost because of its limited capacity. It is to be noted that LAC curve is not a tangent to the minimum points of the SAC curves. When the LAC curve is declining it is tangent to the falling portions of the short run cost curves and when the LAC curve is rising it is tangent to the rising portions of the short run cost curves. Thus for producing output less than "OQ" at the lowest possible unit cost the firm will construct the relevant plant and operate it at less than its full capacity, i.e., at less than its minimum average cost of production. On the other hand for output larger than OQ the firm will construct a plant and operate it beyond its optimum capacity. "OQ" is the optimum output. This is because "OQ" is being produced at the minimum point of LAC and corresponding SAC i.e., SAC4. Other plants are either used at less than their full capacity or more than their full capacity. Only SAC4 is being operated at the minimum point. Long run average cost curve is often called a planning curve because a firm plans to produce any output in the long run by choosing a plant on the long run average cost curve corresponding to the given output. The long run average cost curve helps the firm in the choice of the size of the plant for producing a specific output at the least possible cost.

Explanation of the "U" shape of the long run average cost curve: As has been seen in the diagram LAC curve is a "U" shape curve. This shape of LAC curve depends upon the returns to scale. As discussed earlier, as the firm expands, returns to scale increase. After a range of constant returns to scale, the returns to scale finally decrease. On the same line, the LAC curve first declines and then finally rises. Increasing returns to scale cause fall in the long run average cost and decreasing returns to scale result in increase in long run average cost. Falling long run average cost and increasing economies to scale result from internal and external economies of scale and rising long run average cost and diminishing returns to scale from internal and external diseconomies of scale (economies of scale have been discussed earlier at the relevant place).

The long run average cost curve initially falls with increase in output and after a certain point it rises making a boat shape. Long-run Average cost (LAC) curve is also called the planning curve of the firm as it helps in choosing a plant on the decided level of output. The long-run average cost curve is called Envelope curve, because it envelopes or supports a family of short run average cost curves from below. The above figure depicting long-run average cost curve is arrived at on the basis of traditional economic analysis. It is flattened 'U' shaped. This type of curve could exist only when the state of technology remains constant. But the empirical evidence shows that the state of technology changes in the long-run. Therefore, modern firms face 'L-shaped' cost curve than 'u-shaped'. The L shaped cost curve is given below. According to the diagram, over AB range, the curve is perfectly flat. Over this range all sizes of plant have the same minimum cost.

Long Run Average cost (LRAC) curve 'L'- shaped curve

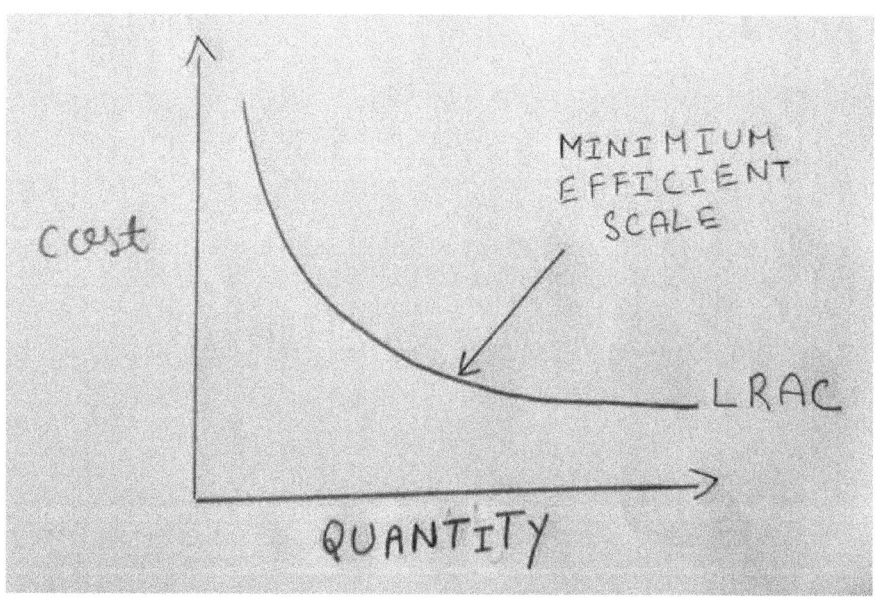

Chapter 5

Production Analysis

Structure:

5.1 Introduction

5.2 Meaning of Production and Production Function

5.3 Uses of Production Function

5.4 Types of Production Function

5.5 Production Isoquant

5.6 Types of Isoquant

5.7 Derivation of Smooth Convex Isoquant

5.8 Properties of Isoquants

5.9 Isocost

5.10 Producers Equilibrium or Optimal Combination of Inputs

5.11 Managerial Uses of Production Function

5.12 Production Function with One Variable Input Case (Short Run Production Function)

5.13 The Law of Variable Proportions (Long Run Production Function)

5.14 Economies of Scale

5.15 Economies of Scope

5.16 Summary

5.17 Terminal Questions

5.1 Introduction

Production functions and cost functions are the cornerstones of business and managerial economics. A production function is a mathematical relationship that captures the essential features of the technology by means of which an organisation metamorphoses resources such as land, labour and capital into goods or services such as steel or cement. It is the economist's distillation of the salient information contained in the engineer's blueprints. Mathematically, let Y denote the quantity of a single output produced by the quantities of inputs denoted (x1... xn). Then the production function f (x1,..xn) describes how a given output can be produced by an infinite combinations of inputs (x1,.., xn), given the technology in use. Several important features of the structure of the technology are captured by the shape of the production function. Relationships among inputs include the degree of substitutability or complementarily among pairs of inputs, as well as the ability to aggregate groups of inputs into a shorter list of input aggregates. Relationships between output and the inputs include economies of scale and the technical efficiency with which inputs are utilised to produce a given output.

5.2 Meaning of Production Function

Synonymous to the demand theory that pivots around the concept of the demand function, the theory of production revolves around the concept of the production function. A production function can be an equation, table or graph presenting the maximum amount of a commodity that a firm can produce from a given set of inputs during a period of time.

The concept of production function portrays the ways in which the factors of production are combined by a firm to produce different levels of output. More specifically, it shows the maximum volume of physical output available from a given set of inputs or the minimum set of inputs necessary to produce any given level of output. The production function comprises an engineering or technical relation, because the relation between inputs and outputs is a technical one. The production function is determined by a given state of technology. When the technology improves the production function changes, because the new production function can yield greater output from the given inputs or smaller inputs will be enough to produce a given level of output. Further, the production function incorporates the idea of efficiency. Thus, production function is not any relation between inputs and outputs, but a relation in which a given set of inputs produces a maximum output. Therefore, the production function includes all the technically efficient methods of producing an output.

A method or process of production is a combination of inputs required for the production of output. A method of production is technically efficient to any other method if it uses less of at least one factor and no more of the other factors as compared with another method.

Example: Technically Efficient Method of Production

Let us suppose that commodity X is produced by two methods by using labour and capital:

Factor Inputs	Method A	Method B
Labour	3	4
Capital	4	4

In the above example, method B is inefficient compared to method A because method B uses more of labour and same amount of capital as compared to method A. A profit maximising firm will not be interested in improvident or inefficient methods of production. If method A uses less of one factor and more of the other factor as compared with any other method C, then method A and C are not directly comparable. For example, let us suppose that a commodity is produced by two methods:

Factor Inputs	Method A	Method C
Labour	3	2
Capital	4	5

In the above example, both methods A and C are technically efficient and are included in the production function, which one of them would be chosen depends on the prices of factors. The choice of any particular technique from a set of technically efficient techniques (or methods) is an economic one, based on prices and not a technical one. In a production function, the dependent variable is the output and the independent variables are the inputs. Thus, the production function can be expressed as

$$Q = f(N, L, K, E, T)$$

Where = Quantity Produced, N = Natural resources, L = Labour, K = Capital, E = Entrepreneur or organizer and T = Technology.

For simplicity, only the inputs of labour and capital are considered independent variables in a production function. Normally, land does not enter the production function explicitly because of the implicit assumption that land does not impose any restriction on production. However, labour and capital enter production explicitly. A simple specification of a production function is

$$Q = f(L, K)$$

Where Q, as above, is the output, L and K are the quantities of labour and capital and f shows the functional relation between the inputs and output. The production function is based on an implicit assumption that the technology is given. This is because an improvement in technical knowledge will lead to larger output from the use of same quantity of inputs.

5.3 Uses Of Production Function

The production function can have various uses. It can be used to compute the least cost factor combination for a given output or the maximum output combination for a given cost. Knowledge of production function may be helpful in deciding on the value of employing a variable factor in the production process. As long as the marginal revenue productivity of a variable factor exceeds its price, it will be profitable to increase its use. When the marginal revenue productivity of the factor becomes equal to its price the additional employment of the factor should be stopped. Since, the production function shows the returns to scale it will help in the decision making. If the returns to scale are diminishing, it is not worthwhile to increase production. The opposite will be true if the returns to scale are increasing.

5.4 Types Of Production Function

Production function is of two different forms:

- The Fixed Proportion Production Function
- The Variable Proportion Production Function

These can be explained as follows:

1. Fixed Proportion Production Function

A fixed proportion production function is one in which the technology requires a fixed combination of inputs, say capital and labour, to produce a given level of output. There is only one way in which the factors may be combined to produce a given level of output efficiently. In this type of production, there is no possibility of substitution between the factors of production.

The fixed proportion production function is illustrated by isoquants which are 'L' shaped or 'right angle' shaped. This is shown in Figure below.

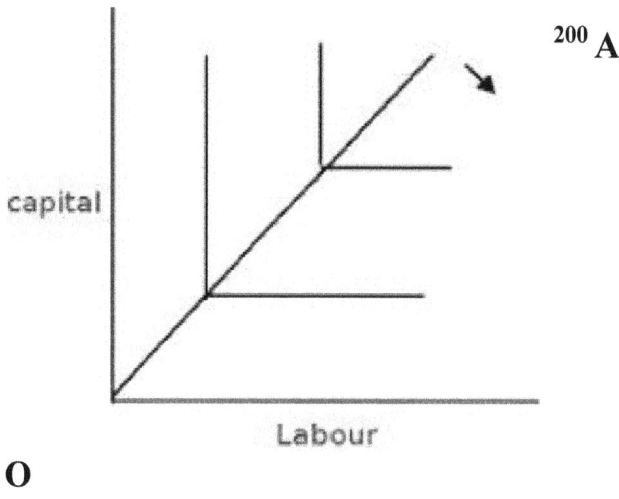

In this diagram OR represents the fixed capital ratio and two units of capital and three units of labour produce 100 units of output. In order to produce 200 units of output the factor units have to be doubled. In other words four units of capital and six units of labour are required. A-B are isoquant curves. An isoquant curve is defined as the curve representing different combination of inputs which will yield certain amount of output. In the above diagram isoquant is right angled.

2. Variable Proportions Production Function

The variable proportion production is the most familiar function. In this case, a given level of output can be produced by several alternative combinations of factors of production, say capital and labour. It is assumed that the factors can be combined in infinite number of ways. The common level of output obtained from alternative combinations of capital and labour is given by an isoquant Q in Figure given below:

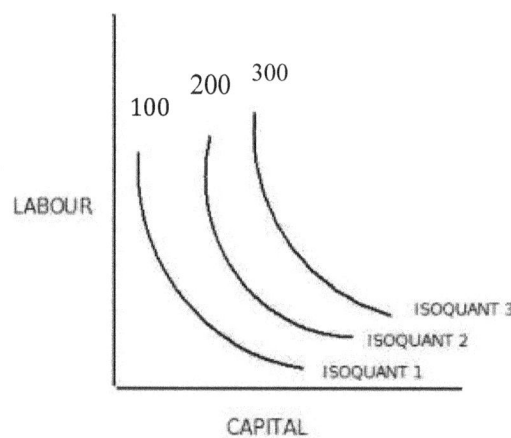

If one input is substituted for another input to produce the same amount of amount of output, then the isoquant curve moves from upwards to the downwards as shown the following diagram. This is called as variable proportions production function.

5.5 Production Isoquant

An isoquant shows all those combinations of factors which produce the same level of output. An isoquant is also known as equal product curve or iso-product curve. There may be different combination of inputs. Each combination is called a scale of preference. Each scale when applied will produce the same quantity of output. Thus,"Iso-Quant" (which means equal quantity) curve indicates that each curve will have different scales of preference of input which can produce the same quantity of ouput.

5.6 Types of Isoquants

The isoquant may have various shapes depending on the degree of substitutability of factors:

1. Linear Isoquant: In this case, the isoquant would be straight lines as in Figure. This type assumes perfect substitutability of factors of production. In this case, labour and capital are perfect substitutes, that is, the rate at which labour can be substituted for capital in production is constant.

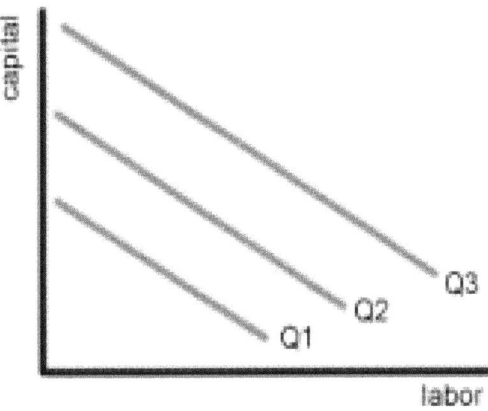

This isoquant evinces that a given commodity may be produced by using only capital or only labour or by an infinite combination of labour and capital. At point A on the isoquant the level of output can be produced with capital alone (i.e. without labour). Similarly, point B indicates that the same level of output can be produced with labour alone (i.e. without any capital). This is unrealistic because capital and labour are not perfectly substitutable.

2. **Right Angled Isoquant:** This assumes zero substitutability of the factors of production. There is only one method of producing any one commodity. In this case, the isoquant takes the form of a right angle as in Figure.

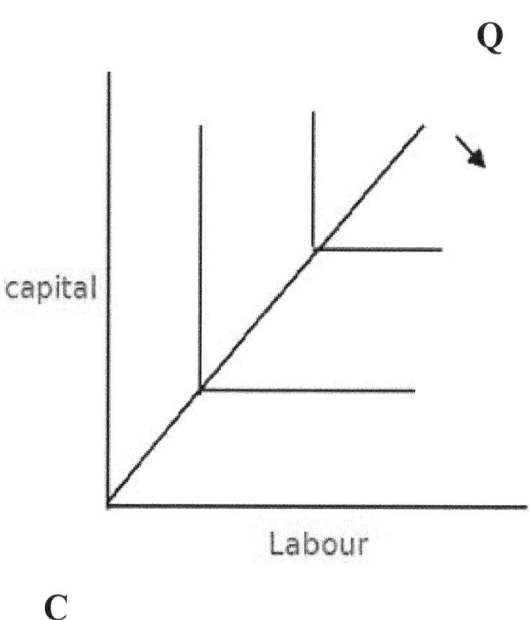

C

In this case, labour and capital are perfect complements, that is, labour and capital must be used in fixed proportion shown by point C. The output can be increased only by increasing both the quantity of labour and capital in the same proportion depicted at the point C. This isoquant is called input-output isoquant or Leontief isoquant after Leontief, who invented the input-output analysis.

Kinked Isoquant: This isoquant assumes only limited substitutability of capital and labour. There are only a few processes for producing any one commodity. This is shown in Figure where A, B, C and D show the production process and Q is the kinked isoquant. In this case, the O substitutability of factors is possible only at the kinks.

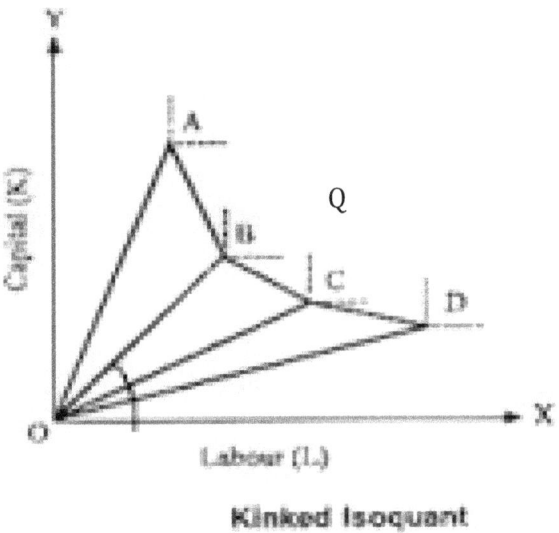

Kinked Isoquant

This is more realistic type of isoquant because engineers, managers and production executives consider the production process as a discrete rather than continuous process.

3. **Smooth Convex Isoquant:** This type of isoquant assumes continuous substitutability of capital and labour over a certain range, beyond which the factors cannot substitute each other. This is shown in Figure.

CAPITAL

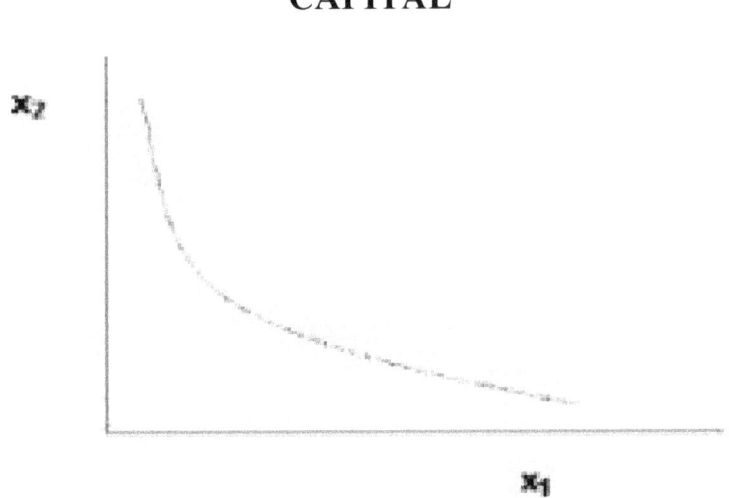

LABOUR

The traditional economic theory has adopted this isoquant for analysis since it is uncomplicated. Further, this is an approximation to the more realistic form of a kinked isoquant because as the number of process become infinite, the isoquant becomes a smooth curve. Therefore, the properties of this isoquant are explained in detail below.

5.7 Derivation of Smooth Convex Isoquant

It is assumed that each of the different combinations of labour and capital shown in Table produces the same level of output, that is, 100 units. The combinations are such that if one factor is increased the other factor is decreased and vice versa. All these combinations are technically efficient.

Table: Various Combinations of Labour and Capital to Produce 100 Units of Output.

Factor Combination	Capital	Labour
A	1	20
B	2	16
C	5	4

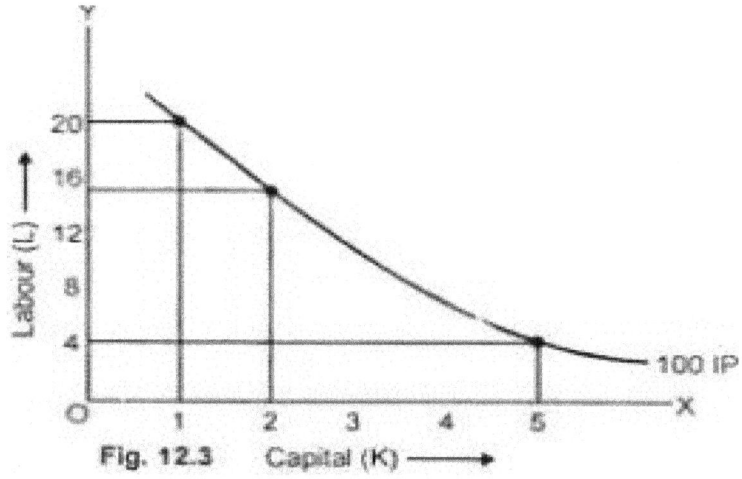

Fig. 12.3

If we plot all these combinations and join them we obtain a curve IP. This is shown in the figure. The curve IP is the isoquant or equal product curve. It shows all those combinations of labour and capital which, with a given technology, produce 100 units of output. Thus, an isoquant is the locus of all those sublimations of labour and capital, which yield the same level of output. In other words, an isoquant includes all the technically efficient methods of producing a given level of output. **Isoquant Map**

We can label isoquants in physical units of output without any difficulty. Since, each isoquant represents a specified level of output it is possible to say by how much the output is greater or lesser on one isoquant than on other. This is explained by an isoquant map shown in Figure.

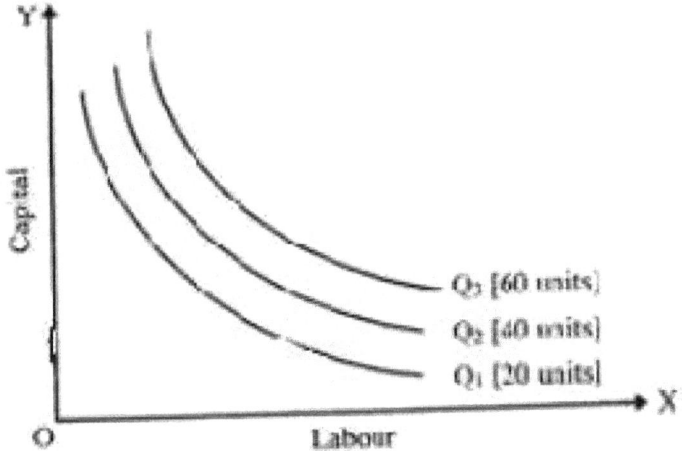

It shows that the output is 20 units, 40 units and 60 units on isoquants Q1, Q2 and Q3 respectively. Thus, on isoquant Q2 the output is 20 units more than on isoquant Q1; and on isoquant Q3 the output is 40 units more than on isoquant Q1. So, an isoquant map facilitates not only measurement of the physical quantities of output but also comparison the size of output between the various isoquants. In theory, an isoquant map contains an infinite number of isoquants. This is because the response of output to infinite changes in factors is assumed to be continuous.

5.8 Properties Of Isoquants

The important properties of isoquants are the following:

1. **Isoquants slope downwards to the right:** It means that, in order to keep the output constant; when the amount of one factor is increased the quantity of other factor must be reduced. An upward sloping isoquant demonstrates that a given product can be produced with less of both the factors of production. An entrepreneur, who is maximising profits, would not use any combinations of factors shown on an upward sloping portion of an isoquant. Therefore, the points on the upward sloping portion of an isoquant cannot represent an equilibrium position. Similarly, a horizontal or vertical range of an isoquant cannot also represent a possible position of equilibrium. In this case, the same output could be obtained at a reduced cost by reducing the amount of one of the factors. Thus, isoquants slope downwards to the right as in figure.

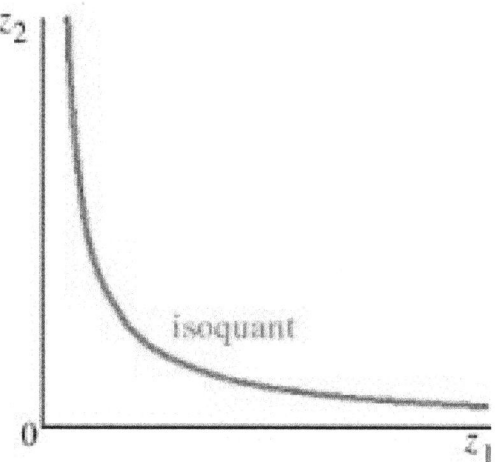

2. **Isoquants are convex to the origin:** The slope, at any point of an isoquant, is negative. Its numerical value measures the marginal rate of technical substitution between labour and capital. It equals the ratio of the marginal product of labour to the marginal product of capital. Thus, the slope of an isoquant is Where ΔK is the change in capital, ΔL is the change in labour, MRTSLK is the marginal rate of technical substitution of labour for capital, MPL is the marginal product of labour and MPK is the marginal product of capital. The convexity of isoquant

means that as we move down the curve less and less of capital is given up for an additional unit of labour so as to keep constant the level of output. This can be observed from the Figure.

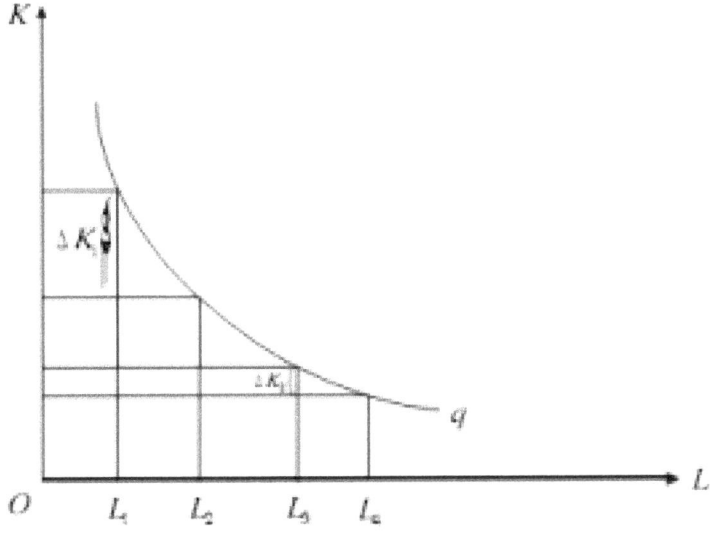

Curvature of an Iso-quant

It can be seen from the figure above that as we increase labour at a constant rate the amount of capital given up (_K) for an additional unit of labour goes on falling. Thus, the convexity of the isoquant shows that the marginal rate of technical substitution of labour for capital is diminishing.

3. **Isoquants do not intersect:** By definition isoquants, like indifference curves, can never cut each other. If they cut each other it would be a logical contradiction.

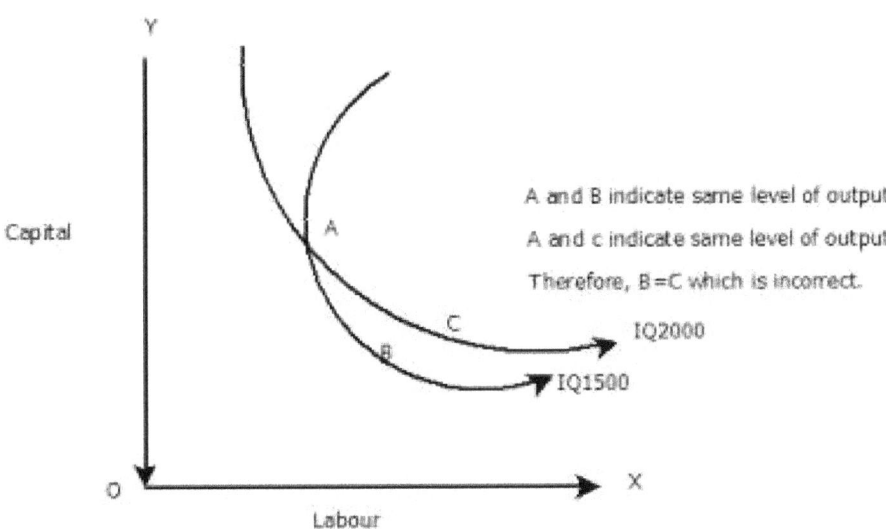

Isoquants cannot touch either axis: If an isoquant touches any axis, as in Figure it would mean that the output can be produced with the help of one factor. It is unrealistic because output cannot be produced only by labour or capital alone.

5.9 Isocost

In economics, an isocost line represents all combinations of inputs which cost the same total amount. Although, similar to the budget constraint in consumer theory, the use of the isocost line pertains to cost-minimisation in production, as opposed to utility maximisation. For the two production inputs, labour and capital, with fixed unit costs of the inputs, the equation of the isocost line is Where w represents the wage rate of labour, r represents the interest rate of capital, K is the amount or units of capital used, L is the amount of labour used and C is the total cost-

$$r K + w L$$

Where w represents the wage rate of labour, r represents the interest rate of capital, K is the amount or units of capital used, L is the amount of labour used and C is the total cost of acquiring these inputs. The absolute value of the slope of the isocost line, with capital plotted vertically and labour plotted horizontally, equals the ratio of the prices of inputs of labour and capital. The isocost line is combined with the isoquant map to determine the optimal production. This optimality is arrived at a point where an isoquant and the isocost curves are tangent to each other. It ensures that the firm attains the highest level of possible output with a given isocost line. Consequently, the output is produced at with least cost or most efficiently. This tangency can also be interpreted as one where the slopes of the isoquant and the isocost are equal. This entails that tangency ensures that the marginal productivities of the two inputs are proportional to the ratios of the prices of the two inputs. Specifically, the point of tangency between an isoquant and an isocost line gives the lowest-cost combination of inputs that can produce the level of output associated with that.

5.10 Producers Equilibrium or Optimal Combination of Inputs

The analysis of production function has shown that alternative combinations of factors of production, which are technically efficient, can be used to produce a given level of output. Of these, the firm will have to choose that combination of factors which will cost it the least. In this way the firm can maximise its profits. The choice of any particular method from a set of technically efficient methods is an economic one and it is based on the prices of factors of production at a particular time. The firm can maximise its profits either by maximising the level of output for a given cost or by minimising the cost of producing a given output. In either case, the factors will have to be employed in optimal combination at which the cost of production will be minimum. There are two ways to determine the least cost combination of factors to produce a given output. That is,

- Finding the total cost of factor combinations
- Geometrical method

1. Finding the Total cost of Factor Combinations

Here we try to find the total cost of each factor combination and choose the one which has the least cost. The cost of each factor combination is found by multiplying the price of each factor by its quantity and then summing it for all inputs. This is illustrated in Table

Technique	Capital	Labour	Capital Cost	Labour Cost	Total
1	2	3	4	5	6
A	6	10	500*6=3000	400*10=4000	7000
B	2	14	500*2=1000	400*14=5600	6600

It is assumed that 100 pairs of shoes are produced per week and the price of capital and the wage of labour are Rs. 500 and Rs. 400 per week respectively. In order to simplify the analysis, we assume that there are only two technically efficient methods of producing shoes and they are labelled A and B. The table demonstrates that the total cost of producing 100 pairs of shoes is Rs. 7000 per week using technique A and Rs. 6600 per week using technique B. The firm will choose technique B, which is an economically efficient (or lowest cost) production technique at the factor prices assumed in the above example. If either of the factor prices alters the equilibrium proportion of the factors will also change so as to use less of those factors that display a price rise. Therefore, we will have a new optimal combination of factors. This can again be found out by calculating the cost of different factor combinations with the new factor prices and choosing the one that costs the least.

2. Geometrical method

The second and a more general way to determine the least cost combination of factors is geometrical in essence. It is done with the help of isoquant map and isocost line. In order to determine the least cost factor combination or the maximum output for a given cost, we have to.

a) Isoquant Map

An isoquant map shows all the possible combinations of labour and capital that can produce different levels of output. The isoquant closer to the origin denotes a lower level of output. The slope of isoquant is =

$$MRTS_{LK} = MP_L / MP_K$$

The isocost line shows various combinations of labour and capital that the firm could buy for a given amount of money at the given factor prices. This is explained in Figure. Isocost line is a locus of combination of labour and capital which, given the prices of labour and capital, could be bought for a given amount of money. The slope of the isocost line is equal to the ratio of the factor prices, that is, the slope of isocost line. Similar iso-cost lines can be drawn for different sums of money.

Slope of Isocost Line

If factor cost change slope of Isocost line will change. Let us assume that with a given amount of money and the prices of labour and capital, the iso-cost line is AC in Figure. If the price of labour falls the firm could hire more than OC amount of labour for the same amount of money. If we assume that the firm could hire only OC, amount of labour then the slope of isocost line changes to AC1. On the other hand if the price of labour rises, the firm could hire less than OC amount of labour. If we assume that the firm could hire only OC2 amount of labour then the slope of iso-cost line changes to AC2. Thus, the iso-cost line depends upon 2 factors: (i) prices of factors of production (ii) the amount of money which the firm can spend on the factors. A change in the amount of money will shift the Iso-cost lines as in but the slope of iso-cost lines remains constant. A change in factor prices, for example labour will change the slope of iso-cost lines.

Optimal Input Combination for Minimising Cost

In this case, the firm has to produce the given output with the minimum cost. The single isoquant Q denotes the desired level of output. There is a family of isocost lines AB, CD, EF, and GH. The isocost lines are parallel because the factor prices are assumed to be constant and therefore, all the iso-cost lines have the same slope.

The firm minimises its cost at the point 'Q' where the isoquant P is tangent to the isocost line CD. The optimal combination of factors is ON and OM. The optimal combination takes place at the point 'Q' where the given output can be produced at the least cost. Points below 'Q' are desirable but are not attainable for output P. Points above 'Q' are on higher iso-cost lines and they show higher costs. Hence, the point 'Q' is the least cost point and it is the lowest cost combination of factors for producing the output P. It is produced by ON amount of capital and OM amount of labour. At the point of tangency, that is, at point 'Q', the slope of isocost line is equal to the slope of the isoquant. This is the first condition for the equilibrium. The second condition is that the isoquant should be convex to the origin at the point of equilibrium. Thus at the point 'e' the ratio of marginal product of two factors is equal to the ratio of their factor prices.

Optimal Input Combination For Maximization of Output

The equilibrium conditions of the firm are identical to the above situation that is, the iso-cost line should be tangent to the highest possible isoquant and the isoquant must be convex. However, the present problem is conceptually different. In this case the firm has to maximise its output for a given cost.

The firm's cost constraint is given by the iso-cost line NM. The maximum level of output that the firm can produce is IQ2 because the point 'e' lies on the isoquant IQ2. The point 'e' is the equilibrium point because at this point the iso-cost line NM is tangent to the isoquant IQ2. Other points on the isocost line that is A and B, lie on a lower isoquant IQ1. Points to the right of 'e' indicate higher levels of output which are desirable, but are not attainable due to the cost constraint.

Hence, IQ2 is the maximum output possible for the given cost. The optimal combination of factors is OK0 and OL0.

The above analysis shows that the optimal combination of inputs needed for a firm to minimise the cost of producing a given level of output or to maximise the output for a given cost outlay is given at the tangency point of an isoquant and is cost line. The above analysis is based on constant factor prices. If the factor prices change, the firm will choose another factor combination that will minimize the cost of production for the given output or maximize the level of output for a given cost.

5.11 Managerial Uses of Production Function

Though production function may appear as highly abstract and unrealistic, in reality, it is both logical and useful. It is of immense utility to the managers and executives in the decision making process at the firm level. There are several possible combinations of inputs and decision makers have to choose the most appropriate among them. The following are some of the important uses of production function.

1. It can be used to calculate or work out the least cost input combination for a given output or the maximum output-input combination for a given cost.

2. It is useful in working out an optimum, and economic combination of inputs for getting a certain level of output. The utility of employing a unit of variable factor input in the production process can be better judged with the help of production function. Additional employment of a variable factor input is desirable only when the marginal revenue productivity of that variable factor input is greater than or equal to cost of employing it in an organization.

3. Production function also helps in making long run decisions. If returns to scale are increasing, it is wise to employ more factor units and increase production. If returns to scale are diminishing, it is unwise to employ more factor inputs & increase production. Managers will be indifferent whether to increase or decrease production, if production is subject to constant returns to scale.

Thus, production function helps both in the short run and long run decision - making process.

5.12 Production Function with One Variable Input Case (Short Run Production Function)

Short run is a period of time in which only the variable factors can be varied while fixed factors like plants, machineries, top management etc would remain constant. Time available at the disposal of a producer to make changes in the quantum of factor inputs is very much limited in the short run. Long run is a period of time where in the producer will have adequate time to make any sort of changes in the factor combinations.

It is necessary to note that production function is assumed to be a continuous function, i.e. it is assumed that a change in any of the variable factors produces corresponding changes in the output. Generally speaking, there are two types of production functions. They are as follows:

1. Short Run Production Function

In this case, the producer will keep all fixed factors as constant and change only a few variable factor inputs. In the short run, we come across two kinds of production functions:

i) Quantities of all inputs both fixed and variable will be kept constant and only one variable input will be varied. For example, Law of Variable Proportions.

ii) Quantities of all factor inputs are kept constant and only two variable factor inputs are varied. For example, Iso-Quants and Iso-Cost curves.

2. Long Run Production Function

In this case, the producer will vary the quantities of all factor inputs, both fixed as well as variable in the same proportion. For Example, The laws of returns to scale.

Each firm has its own production function which is determined by the state of technology, managerial ability, organizational skills etc of a firm. If there are any improvements in them, the old production function is disturbed and a new one takes its place. It may be in the following manner –

i) The quantity of inputs may be reduced while the quantity of output may remain same.

ii) The quantity of output may increase while the quantity of inputs may remain same.

iii) The quantity of output may increase and quantity of inputs may decrease.

5.13 The Law of Variable Proportions (Long Run Production Function)

This law is one of the most fundamental laws of production. It gives us one of the key insights to the working out of the most ideal combination of factor inputs. All factor inputs are not available in plenty. Hence, in order to expand the output, scarce factors must be kept constant and variable factors are to increased in greater quantities. Additional units of a variable factor on the fixed factors will certainly mean a variation in output. The law of variable proportions or the law of non proportional output will explain how variation in one factor input give place for variations in outputs.

The law can be stated as the following. **As the quantity of different units of only one factor input is increased to a given quantity of fixed factors, beyond a particular point, the marginal, average and total output eventually decline.**

The law of variable proportions is the new name for the famous **"Law of Diminishing Returns"** of classical economists. This law is stated by various economists in the following manner – According to Prof. Benham, **"As the proportion of one factor in a combination of factors is increased, after a point, first the marginal and then the average product of that factor will diminish"**

The same idea has been expressed by Prof.Marshall in the following words. An increase in the quantity of a variable factor added to fixed factors, at the end results in a less than proportionate increase in the amount of product, given technical conditions.

Assumptions of the Law

1. Only one variable factor unit is to be varied while all other factors should be kept constant. tor inputs.

Illustration

A hypothetical production schedule is worked out to explain the operation of the law. Fixed factors = 1 Acre of land + Rs 5000-00 capital. Variable factor = labor.

Units of Variable inputs (Labor)	TP in Units	AP in Units	MP in Units
1	10	10	10
2	24	12	14
3	39	13	15
4	52	13	13
5	60	12	8
6	66	11	6
7	70	10	4
8	72	9	2
9	72	8	0
10	70	7	-2

Total Product or Output:

(TP) It is the output derived from all factors units, both fixed & variable employed by the producer. It is also a sum of marginal output.

Average Product or Output: (AP) It can be obtained by dividing total output by the number of variable factors employed.

Marginal Product or Output: (MP) It is the output derived from the employment of an additional unit of variable factor unit

Trends in output

From the table, one can observe the following tendencies in the TP, AP, & MP.

1. Total output goes on increasing as long as MP is positive. It is the highest when MP is zero and TP declines when MP becomes negative.

2. MP increases in the beginning, reaches the highest point and diminishes at the end.

3. AP will also have the same tendencies as the MP. In the beginning MP will be higher than AP but at the end AP will be higher than MP.

In the above diagram along with OX axis, we measure the amount of variable factors employed and along OY - axis, we measure TP, AP & MP. From the diagram it is clear that there are III stages.

Stage Number I. The Law of Increasing Returns

The total output increases at an increasing rate (More than proportionately) up to the point P because corresponding to this point F the MP is rising and reaches its highest point. After the point F, MP decline and as such TP increases gradually. The first stage comes to an end at the point where MP curve cuts the AP curve when the AP is maximum at S.

The I stage is called as the law of increasing returns on account of the following reasons.

1. The proportion of fixed factors is greater than the quantity of variable factors. When the producer increases the quantity of variable factor, intensive and effective utilization of fixed factors become possible leading to higher output.

2. When the producer increases the quantity of variable factor, output increases due to the complete utilization of the "Indivisible Factors".

3. As more units of the variable factor is employed, the efficiency of variable factors will go up because it creates more opportunity for the introduction of division of labor and specialization resulting in higher output.

Stage Number II. The Law of Diminishing Returns

In this case as the quantity of variable inputs is increased to a given quantity of fixed factors, output increases less than proportionately. In this stage, the T.P increases at a diminishing rate since both AP & MP are declining but they are positive. The II stage comes to an end at the point where TP is the highest at the point H and MP is zero at the point M. It is known as the stage of "Diminishing Returns" because both the AP & MP of the variable factor continuously fall during this stage. It is only in this stage, the firm is maximizing its total output.

Diminishing returns arise due to the following reasons:

1. The proportion of variable factors is greater than the quantity of fixed factors. Hence, both AP & MP decline.

2. Total output diminishes because there is a limit to the full utilization of indivisible factors and introduction of specialization. Hence, output declines.

3. Diseconomies of scale will operate beyond the stage of optimum production.

4. Imperfect substitutability of factor inputs is another cause. Up to certain point substitution is beneficial. Once optimum point is reached, the fixed factors cannot be compensated by the variable factor. Diminishing returns are bound to appear as long as one or more factors are fixed and cannot be substituted by the others.

The III Stage The Stage of Negative Returns:

In this case, as the quantity of variable input is increased to a given quantity of fixed factors, output becomes negative. During this stage, TP starts diminishing, AP continues to diminish and MP becomes negative. The negative returns are the result of excessive quantity of variable factors to a constant quantity of fixed factors. Hence, output declines. The proverb "Too many cooks spoil the broth" and " Too much is too bad" aptly applies to this stage. Generally, the III stage is a theoretical possibility because no producer would like to come to this stage.

The producer being rational will not select either the stage I (because there is opportunity for him to increase output by employing more units of variable factor) or the III stage (because the MP is negative). The stage I & III are described as NON-Economic Region or Uneconomic Region.

Hence, the producer will select the II stage (which is described as the most economic region) where he can maximize the output. The II stage represents the range of rational production decision.

It is clear that in the above example, the most ideal or optimum combination of factor units = 1 Acre of land+ Rs. 5000 - 00 capital and 9 laborers. All the 3 stages together constitute the law of variable proportions. Since the second stage is the most important, in practice we normally refer this law as the law of Diminishing Returns.

Long Run Production Function [Change In All Factor Inputs In The Same Proportion]

Laws of Returns to Scale

The concept of returns to scale is a long run phenomenon. In this case, we study the change in output when all factor inputs are changed or made available in required quantity. An increase in scale means that all factor inputs are increased in the same proportion. In returns to scale, all the necessary factor inputs are increased or decreased to the same extent so that whatever the scale of production, the proportion among the factors remains the same.

Three Phases of Returns to Scale

Generally speaking, we study the behavior pattern of output when all factor inputs are increased in the same proportion under returns to scale. Many economists have questioned the validity of returns to scale on the ground that all factor inputs cannot be increased in the same proportion and the proportion between the factor inputs cannot be kept uniform. But in some cases, it is possible that all factor inputs can be changed in the same proportion and the output is studied when the input is doubled or tripled or increased five-fold or ten-fold. An ordinary person may think that when the quantity of inputs is increased 10 times, output will also go up by 10 times. But it may or may not happen as expected.

It may be noted that when the quantity of inputs are increased in the same proportion, the scale of output or returns to scale may be either more than equal, equal or less than equal. Thus, when the scale of output is increased, we may get increasing returns, constant returns or diminishing returns. When the quantity of all factor inputs are increased in a given proportion and output increases more than proportionately, then the returns to scale are said to be increasing; when the output increases in the same proportion, then the returns to scale are said to be constant; when the output increases less than proportionately, then the returns to scale are said to be diminishing.

SL.NO	SCALE	TOTAL PRODUCTS IN UNITS	MARGINAL PRODUCTS IN UNITS
1	1 Acre of land + 3 labor	5	5
2	8 Acre of land + 17 labor	12	7
3	3 Acre of land + 7 labor	21	9
4	4 Acre of land + 9 labor	32	11
5	5 Acre of land + 11 labor	43	11
6	6 Acre of land + 13 labor	54	11
7	7 Acre of land + 15 labor	63	9

| 8 | 8 Acre of land + 17 labor | 70 | 7 |

It is clear from the table that the quantity of land and labor (Scale) is increasing in the same proportion, i.e. by 1 acre of land and 2 units of labor throughout in our example. The output increases more than proportionately when the producer is employing 4 acres of land and 9 units of labor. Output increases in the same proportion when the quantity of land is 5 acres and 11units of labor and 6 acres of land and 13 units of labor. In the later stages, when he employs 7 & 8 acres of land and 15 & 17 units of labor, output increases less than proportionately. Thus, one can clearly understand the operation of the three phases of the laws of returns to scale with the help of the table.

Diagrammatic representation

In the diagram, it is clear that the marginal returns curve slope upwards from R to P, indicating increasing returns to scale. The curve is horizontal from P to Q indicating constant returns to scale and from Q to S, the curve slope downwards from left to right indicating the operation of diminishing to returns to scale.

Increasing returns to scale is said to operate when the producer is increasing the quantity of all factors [scale] in a given proportion, output increases more than proportionately. For example, when the quantity of all inputs are increased by 10%, and output increases by 15%, then we say that increasing returns to scale is operating. In order to explain the operation of this law, an equal product map has been drawn with the assumption that only two factors X and Y are required. In the diagram, Factor X is represented along OX- axis and factor Y is represented along OY axis. The scale line OP is a straight line passing through the origin on the Iso Quant map indicating the increase in scale as we move upward. The scale line OP represent different quantities of inputs where the proportion between factor X and factor Y is remains constant. When the scale is increased from A to B, the return increases from 100 units of output to 200 units. The scale line OP passing through origin is called as the "Expansion path". Any line passing through the origin will indicate the path of expansion or increase in scale with definite proportion between the two factors. It is very clear that the increase in the quantities of factor X and Y [scale] is small as we go up the scale and the output is larger. The distance between each Iso Quant curve is progressively diminishing. It implies that in order to get an increase in output by another 100 units, a producer is employing lesser quantities of inputs and his production cost is declining. Thus, the law of increasing returns to scale is operating.

Causes for Increasing Returns to Scale

Increasing returns to scale operate in a firm on account of several reasons. Some of the most important ones are as follows:

1. Wider scope for the use of latest tools, equipments, machineries, techniques etc to increase production and reduce cost per unit.

2. Large-scale production leads to full and complete utilization of indivisible factor inputs leading to further reduction in production cost.

3. As the size of the plant increases, more output can be obtained at lower cost.

4. As output increases, it is possible to introduce the principle of division of labor and specialization, effective supervision and scientific management of the firm etc would help in reducing cost of operations.

5. As output increases, it becomes possible to enjoy several other kinds of economies of scale like overhead, financial, marketing and risk-bearing economies etc, which is responsible for cost reduction.

Constant Returns to Scale

Constant returns to scale is operating when all factor inputs [scale] are increased in a given proportion, output also increases in the same proportion. When the quantity of all inputs is increased by 10%, and output also increases exactly by 10%, then we say that constant returns to scale are operating. In the diagram, it is clear that the successive Iso Quant curves are equi distant from each other along the scale line OP. It indicates that as the producer increases the quantity of both factor X and Y in a given proportion, output also increases in the same proportion. Economists also describe Constant returns to scale as the Linear homogeneous Production function. It shows that with constant returns to scale, there will be one input proportion which does not change, whatever may be level output.

It is important to note that economies of scale out weigh diseconomies of scale in case of increasing returns to scale.

Causes for Diminishing Returns to Scale

Diminishing Returns to Scale operate due to the following reasons

1. Emergence of difficulties in co-ordination and control.

2. Difficulty in effective and better supervision.

3. Delays in management decisions.

4. Inefficient and mis-management due to over growth and expansion of the firm.

5. Productivity and efficiency declines unavoidably after a point.

Thus, in this case, diseconomies outweigh economies of scale. The result is the operation of diminishing returns to scale. The concept of Returns to Scale helps a producer to work out the most desirable combination of factor inputs so as to maximize his output and minimize his production cost. It also helps him, to increase his production, maintain the same level or decrease it depending on the demand for the product.

5.14 Economies of Scale

The study of economies of scale is associated with large scale production. Today there is a general tendency to organize production on a large scale basis. Mass production of standardized goods has become the order of the day. Large scale production is beneficial and economical in nature. **"The advantages or benefits that accrue to a firm as a result of increase in its scale of production are called "Economies of Scale".** They have close relationship with the size of the firm. They influence the average cost over different ranges of output. They are gain to a firm. They help in reducing production cost and establishing an optimum size of a firm. Thus, they help a lot and go a long way in the development and growth of a firm. According to Prof. Marshall these economies are of two types, viz Internal Economies and External Economics. Now we shall study both of them in detail.

I. Internal Economies or Real Economies

Internal Economies are those economies which arise because of the actions of an individual firm to economize its cost. They arise due to increased division of labor or specialization and complete utilization of indivisible factor inputs. Prof. Cairncross points out that internal economies are open to a single factory or a single firm independently of the actions of other firms. They arise on account of an increase in the scale of output of a firm and cannot be achieved unless output increases. The following are some of the important aspects of internal economies.

1. They arise "with in" or "inside" a firm.
2. They arise due to improvements in internal factors.
3. They arise due to specific efforts of one firm.
4. They are particular to a firm and enjoyed by only one firm.
5. They arise due to increase in the scale of production.
6. They are dependent on the size of the firm.
7. They can be effectively controlled by the management of a firm.
8. They are called as "Business Secrets "of a firm.

Kinds of Internal Economies:

1. Technical Economies

These economies arise on account of technological improvements and its practical application in the field of business. Economies of techniques or technical economies are further subdivided into five heads.

- **a. Economies of superior techniques:** These economies are the result of the application of the most modern techniques of production. When the size of the firm grows, it becomes possible to employ bigger and better types of machinery. The latest and improved techniques give place for specialized production. It is bound to be cost reducing in nature For example, cultivating the land with modern tractors instead of using age old wooden ploughs and bullock carts, use of computers instead of human labor etc.

- **b. Economies of increased dimension:** It is found that a firm enjoys the reduction in cost when it increases its dimension. A large firm avoids wastage of time and economizes its expenditure. Thus, an increase in dimension of a firm will reduce the cost of production. For example, operation of a double decker instead of two separate buses.

- **c. Economies of linked process:** It is quite possible that a firm may not have various processes of production with in its own premises. Also it is possible that different firms through mutual agreement may decide to work together and derive the benefits of linked processes, for example, in diary farming, printing press, nursing homes etc.

- **d. Economies arising out of research and by - products:** A firm can invest adequate funds for research and the benefits of research and its costs can be shared by all other firms. Similarly, a large firm can make use of its wastes and by-products in the most economical manner by producing other products. For example, cane pulp, molasses, and bagasse of sugar factory can be used for the production of paper, varnish, distilleries etc.

e. **Inventory Economies.** Inventory management is a part of better materials management. A big firm can save a lot of money by adopting latest inventory management techniques. For example, Just-In-Time or zero level inventory techniques. The rationale of the Just-In-Time technique is that instead of having huge stocks worth of lakhs and crores of rupees, it can ask the seller of the inputs to supply them just before the commencement of work in the production department each day.

2. Managerial Economies:

They arise because of better, efficient, and scientific management of a firm. Such economies arise in two different ways.

a. **Delegation of details:** The general manager of a firm cannot look after the working of all processes of production. In order to keep an eye on each production process he has to delegate some of his powers or functions to trained or specialized personnel and thus relieve himself for co-ordination, planning and executing the plans. This will enable him to bring about improvements in production process and in bringing down the cost of production.

b. **Functional Specialization:** It is possible to secure economies of large scale production by dividing the work of management into several separate departments. Each department is placed under an expert and the rest of the work is left into the hands of specialists. This will ensure better and more efficient productive management with scientific business administration. This would lead to higher efficiency and reduction in the cost of production.

3. Marketing or Commercial economies:

These economies will arise on account of buying and selling goods on large scale basis at favorable terms. A large firm can buy raw materials and other inputs in bulk at concessional rates. As the bargaining capacity of a big firm is much greater than that of small firms, it can get quantity discounts and rebates. In this way economies may be secured in the purchase of different inputs. A firm can reduce its selling costs also. A large firm can have its own sales agency and channel. The firm can have a separate selling organization, marketing department manned by experts who are well versed in the art of pushing the products in the market. It can follow an aggressive sales promotion policy to influence the decisions of the consumers.

4. Financial Economies

They arise because of the advantages secured by a firm in mobilizing huge financial resources. A large firm on account of its reputation, name and fame can mobilize huge funds from money market, capital market, and other private financial institutions at concessional interest rates. It can borrow from banks at relatively cheaper rates. It is also possible to have large overdrafts from banks. A large firm can float debentures and issue shares and get subscribed by the general public. Another advantage will be that the raw material suppliers, machine suppliers etc., are willing to supply material and components at comparatively low rates, because they are likely to get bulk orders. Thus, a big firm has an edge over small firms in securing sufficient funds more easily and cheaply.

5. Labor Economies

These economies will arise as a result of employing skilled, trained, qualified and highly experienced persons by offering higher wages and salaries. As a firm expands, it can employ a large number of highly talented persons and get the benefits of specialization and division of labor. It can also impart training to existing labor force in order to raise skills, efficiency and productivity of workers. New schemes may be chalked out to speed up the work, conserve the scarce resources, economize the expenditure and save labor time. It can provide better working conditions, promotional opportunities, rest rooms, sports rooms etc, and create facilities like subsidized canteen, crèches for infants, recreations. All these measures will definitely raise the average productivity of a worker and reduce the cost per unit of output.

6. Transport and Storage Economies

They arise on account of the provision of better, highly organized and cheap transport and storage facilities and their complete utilization. A large company can have its own fleet of vehicles or means of transport which are more economical than hired ones. Similarly, a firm can also have its own storage facilities which reduce cost of operations.

7. Over Head Economies

These economies will arise on account of large scale operations. The expenses on establishment, administration, book-keeping, etc, are more or less the same whether production is carried on small or large scale. Hence, cost per unit will be low if production is organized on large scale.

8. Economies of Vertical integration

A firm can also reap this benefit when it succeeds in integrating a number of stages of production. It secures the advantages that the flow of goods through various stages in production processes is more readily controlled. Because of vertical integration, most of the costs become controllable costs which help an enterprise to reduce cost of production.

9. Risk-bearing or survival economies

These economies will arise as a result of avoiding or minimizing several kinds of risks and uncertainties in a business. A manufacturing unit has to face a number of risks in the business. Unless these risks are effectively tackled, the survival of the firm may become difficult. Hence many steps are taken by a firm to eliminate or to avoid or to minimize various kinds of risks. Generally speaking, the risk-bearing capacity of a big firm will be much greater than that of a small firm. Risk is avoided when few firms amalgamate or join together or when competition between different firms is either eliminated or reduced to the minimum or expanding the size of the firm. A large firm secures risk-spreading advantages in either of the four ways or through all of them.

- **Diversification of output** Instead of producing only one particular variety, a firm has to produce multiple products. If there is loss in one item, it can be made good in other items.

- **Diversification of market**: Instead of selling the goods in only one market, a firm has to sell its products in different markets. If consumers in one market desert a product, it can cover the losses in other markets.

- **Diversification of source of supply**: Instead of buying raw materials and other inputs from only one source, it is better to purchase them from different sources. If one person fails to supply, a firm can buy from several sources.

- **Diversification of the process of manufacture**: Instead adopting only one process of production to manufacture a commodity, it is better to use different processes or methods to produce the same commodity so as to avoid the loss arising out of the failure of any one process.

II. External Economies or Pecuniary Economies

External economies are those economies which accrue to the firms as a result of the expansion in the output of whole industry and they are not dependent on the output level of individual firms. These economies or gains will arise on account of the overall growth of an industry or a region or a particular area. They arise due to benefit of localization and specialized progress in the industry or region. Prof. Stonier & Hague points out that external economies are those economies in production which depend on increase in the output of the whole industry rather than increase in the output of the individual firm The following are some of the important aspects of external economies.

1. They arise "outside" the firm.
2. They arise due to improvement in external factors.
3. They arise due to collective efforts of an industry.
4. They are general, common & enjoyed by all firms.
5. They arise due to overall development, expansion & growth of an industry or a region.
6. They are dependent on the size of industry.
7. They are beyond the control of management of a firm.

Kinds of External Economies

1. Economies of concentration or Agglomeration

They arise because in a particular area a very large number of firms which produce the same commodity are established. In other words, this is an advantage which arises from what is called "Localization of Industry". The following benefits of localization of industry is enjoyed by all the firms- provision of better and cheap labor at low or reasonable rates, trained, educated and skilled labor, transport and communication, water, power, raw materials, financial assistance through private and public institutions at low interest rates, marketing facilities, benefits of common repairs, maintenance and service shops, services of specialists or outside experts, better use of by

products and other such benefits. Thus, it helps in reducing the cost of operation of a firm.

2. Economies of Information

These economies will arise as a result of getting quick, latest and up to date information from various sources. Another form of benefit that arises due to localization of industry is economies of information. Since a large number of firms are located in a region, it becomes possible for them to exchange their views frequently, to have discussions with others, to organize lectures, symposiums, seminars, workshops, training camps, demonstrations on topics of mutual interest. Revolution in the field of information technology, expansion in inter-net facilities, mobile phones, e-mails, video conferences, etc. has helped in the free flow of latest information from all parts of the globe in a very short span of time. Similarly, publication of journals, magazines, information papers etc have helped a lot in the dissemination of quick information. Statistical, technical and other market information becomes more readily available to all firms. This will help in developing contacts between different firms. When inter-firm relationship strengthens, it helps a lot to economize the expenditure of a single firm.

3. Economies of Disintegration

These economies will arise as a result of dividing one big unit in to different small units for the sake of convenience of management and administration. When an industry grows beyond a limit, in that case, it becomes necessary to split it in to small units. New subsidiary units may grow up to serve the needs of the main industry. For example, in cotton textiles industry, some firms may specialize in manufacturing threads, a few others in printing, and some others in dyeing and coloring etc. This will certainly enhance the efficiency in the working of a firm and cut down unit costs considerably.

4. Economies of Government Action

These economies will arise as a result of active support and assistance given by the government to stimulate production in the private sector units. In recent years, the government in order to encourage the development of private industries has come up with several kinds of assistance. It is granting tax-concessions, tax-holidays, tax-exemptions, subsidies, development rebates, financial assistance at low interest rates etc. It is quite clear from the above detailed description that both internal and external economies arise on account of large scale production and they are benefits to a firm and cost reducing in nature.

5. Economies of Physical Factors

These economies will arise due to the availability of favorable physical factors and environment. As the size of an industry expands, positive physical environment may help to reduce the costs of all firms working in the industry. For example, Climate, weather conditions, fertility of the soil, physical environment in a particular place may help all firms to enjoy certain physical benefits.

6. Economies of Welfare

These economies will arise on account of various welfare programs under taken by an industry to help its own staff. A big industry is in a better position to provide welfare facilities to the workers. It may get land at concessional rates and procure special facilities from the local governments for setting up housing colonies for the workers. It may also establish health care units, training centers, computer centers and educational institutions of all types. It may grant concessions to its workers. All these measures would help in raising the overall efficiency and productivity of workers.

Diseconomies of Scale

When a firm expands beyond the optimum limit, economies of scale will be converted in to diseconomies of scale. Over growth becomes a burden. Hence, one should not cross the limit. On account of diseconomies of scale, more output is obtained at higher cost of production. The following are some of the main diseconomies of scale leading to all kinds of wastages, indiscipline and rise in production and operating costs.

1. **Financial diseconomies**. . As there is over growth, the required amount of fiancée may not be available to a firm. Consequently, higher interest leading to all kinds of wastages, indiscipline and rise in production and operating costs.

2. **Marketing diseconomies.** Unplanned excess production may lead to mismatch between demand and supply of goods leading to fall in prices. Stocks may pile up, sales may decline leading to fall in revenue and profits.

3. **Technical diseconomies.** When output is carried beyond the plant capacity, per unit cost will certainly go up. There is a limit for division of labor and specialization. Beyond a point, they become negative. Hence, operation costs would go up.

4. **Diseconomies of risk and uncertainty bearing.** If output expands beyond a limit, investment increases. The level of inventory goes up. Sales do not go up correspondingly. Business risks appear in all fields of activities. Supply of factor inputs become inelastic leading to high prices.

5. **Labor diseconomies.** An unwieldy firm may become impersonal. Contact between labor and management may disappear. Workers may demand higher wages and salaries, bonus and other such benefits etc. Industrial disputes may arise. Labor unions may not cooperate with the management. All of them may contribute for higher operation costs.

II. External diseconomies. When several business units are concentrated in only one place or locality, it may lead to congestion,, environmental pollution, scarcity of factor inputs like, raw materials, water, power, fuel, transport and communications etc leading to higher production and operational costs.

Thus, it is very clear that a firm can enjoy benefits of large scale production only up to a limit. Beyond the optimum limit, it is bound to experience diseconomies of scale. Hence, there should be proper check on the growth and expansion of a firm.

Internalization of External Economies

It implies that a firm will convert certain external benefits created by the government or the entire society to its own favor with out making any additional investments. A firm may start a new unit in between two big railway stations or near the air port or near the national high ways or a port so that it can enjoy all the infrastructure benefits. Similarly, a new computer firm can commence its operations where there is 24 hours supply of electricity. Hence, they are also called as privatization of public benefits. Such type of efforts is to be encouraged by the government. **Externalization of Internal Diseconomies**

In this case, a particular firm on account of its regular operations will pass on certain costs on the entire society. A firm instead of taking certain precautionary measures by spending some amount of money will escape and pass on this burden to the government or the society. For example, a firm may throw chemical or industrial wastes, dirt and filth either to open air or rivers leading to environmental pollution. In that case, the government forced to spend more money to clean river water or prevent environmental pollution. This is a clear case of externalized internal diseconomies. It is to be avoided at all costs.

5.15 Economies of Scope

It is a common factor to observe that when a single-product firm expands its volume of output, it would enjoy certain economies of scale. As a result, production cost per unit declines and more output is obtained at lower cost of production. Sometimes they would enjoy certain other external benefits due to the overall improvements in the entire area or city in which operates. Apart from these two types of benefits, we also come across another type of benefits in recent years. They are popularly known as economies of scope.

Economies of scope may be defined as those benefits which arise to a firm when it produces more than one product jointly rather than producing two items separately by two different business units. In this case, the benefits of the joint output of a single firm are greater than the benefits if two products are produced separately by two different firms. Such benefits may arise on account of joint use of production facilities, joint marketing efforts, or use of the same administrative office and staff in an organization. Sometimes, production of one product automatically results in the production of another by-product leading to a reduction in average cost of production.

Economies of scope results in saving production costs. It can be measured with the help of the following equation.

SC= C (Q1) +C (Q2)-C (Q1&Q2) \ C (Q1&Q2)

Where SC = Saving Cost, C Q1 = cost of producing output Q1, C Q2 = cost of producing outputQ2 and C [Q1, Q2] = joint cost of producing both outputs.

Ilustration

A firm produces product A & B separately. Cost of producing 100 units of A is Rs. 8000 – 00 and cost of producing 100 units of B is Rs. 5,000-00. If the firm produces both products A & B jointly, in that case, its total cost would be Rs. 10,000 - 00.

Now one can find out saving cost by substituting the values to the above mentioned formula. SC = 8000+5000-10,000/10,000*3000/10,000 =0.3

In this case, the joint cost [10,000-00] is less than a sum of individual costs [13,000-00]. Thus, a firm can save 3% cost if it produces both products A & B jointly. Hence, the SC is more than zero.

Diseconomies of Scope

Diseconomies of scope may be defined as those disadvantages which occur when cost of producing two products jointly are costlier than producing them individually. In this case, it would be profitable to produce two goods separately than jointly. For example, with the help of same machinery, it is not possible to produce two goods together. It involves buying two different machineries. Hence, production costs would certainly go up in this case.

Difference between Economies of Scale and Economies of Scope

Economies of Scale	Economies of Scope
It is connected with increase and decrease in scale of production	It is connected with increase and decrease in distribution and marketing
It shows change in output of a single product.	It shows change in output of more than one product
It is associated with supply side changes in output.	It is associated with demand side changes in output
It indicates savings in cost owing to increase in volume of output.	It indicates savings in cost due to production of more than one product.

5.16 Summary

In this Module we have discussed about the meaning of production, production function and its managerial uses. Production in economics implies transformation of inputs into outputs for our final consumption. Production function explains the quantitative relationship between the amounts of inputs used to get a particular physical quantity of outputs. The ratios between the two quantities are of great importance to a producer to take his decisions in the production process.

There are two kinds of production functions - short run and long run. In case of short run production function we come across a change in either one or two variable factor inputs while all other inputs are kept constant. The law of variable proportion explain how there will be variations in the quantity of output when there is change in only one variable factor input while all other inputs are kept constant. On the other hand, Iso-Quants and Iso-cost curves explain how there will be changes in output when only two variable inputs are changed while all other inputs are kept constant. Under long run production function, the laws of returns to scale explain changes in output when all inputs, both variable as well as fixed changes in the same proportion.

Economies of scale give information about the various benefits that a firm will get when it goes for large scale production. Economies of scope on the other hand tells us how there will be certain specific advantages when one firm produces more than two products jointly than two or three firms

produce them separately. Diseconomies of scale and diseconomies of scope tells us that there are certain limitations to expansion in output.

5.17 Terminal Questions

1. Define production function and distinguish between short run and long run production function.
2. Discuss the uses of production function.
3. Explain the law of variable proportions.
4. Explain how a product would reach equilibrium position with the help of ISO - Quant's and ISO-Cost curve.
5. Discuss any one laws of returns to scale with example.
6. Explain either various internal or external economies of scale.

◆ ◆ ◆

Chapter 6

Meaning of Market and Market Structure

Structure

6.1 Introduction.

6.2 Case Studies.

6.3 Impact Of The Reforms.

6.4 Conclusion.

6.5 Monopoly.

Market

Generally the term market has come to signify a public place in which goods and services are bought and sold. It is the act or technique of buying and selling. Prof Jevons defines market as "Any- body of persons who are in intimate business relations and carry on extensive transactions in any commodity"

Classification of Market

In Economics, generally the classification is made on the basis of

(a) Area

(b) Time

(c) Nature of Transaction

(d) Regulation

(e) Volume of Business

(f) Types of Competition

On the basis of Area

On the basis of geographical area covered, markets are classified into

a) **Local Markets:** Generally, markets for perishable like butter, eggs, milk, vegetables, etc., will have local markets. Likewise, bulky articles like bricks, sand, stones, etc., will have local markets as the ransport of these over a long distance will be uneconomic.

b) **Regional Markets:** Semi-durable goods command a regional market.

c) **National Markets**: In this market durable goods and industrial items exist

d) **International markets**: The precious commodities like gold, silver etc. are traded in the international market.

On the basis of Time:

Alfred Marshall conceived the 'Time' elements in marketing and this is classified into

a) **Very short period market**: It refers to that type of market in which the commodities are perishable and supply of commodities cannot be changed at all. In a very short-period market, the market supply is almost fixed and it cannot be increased or decreased, because skilled labour, capital and organization are fixed. Commodities like vegetables, flower, fish, eggs, fruits, milk, etc., which are perishable and the supply of which cannot be changed in the very short period come under this category.

b) **Short-period Market**: Short period is a period which is slightly longer than the very short period. In this period, the supply of output will be increased by increasing the employment of variable factors to the given fixed capital equipments.

c) **Long-period Market**: It implies that the time available is adequate for altering the supplies by altering even the fixed factors of production. The supply of commodities may be increased by installing a new plant or machinery and the output adjustments can be made accordingly.

d) **Very long-period or secular period** is one when secular movements are recorded in certain factors over a period of time. The period is very long. The factors include the size of the population, capital supply, supply of raw materials etc.

On the basis of Nature of Transactions

a) Spot Market: Spot transactions or spot markets refer to those markets where goods are physically transacted on the spot.

b) Future Market: It is related to those transactions which involve contracts of the future date.

On the basis of Regulation:

a) **Regulated Market:** In this market, transactions are statutorily regulated so as to put an end to unfair practices. Such markets may be established for specific products or a group of products. Eg. stock exchange.

b) **Unregulated Market**: It is also called as free market as there are no restrictions on the transactions.

On the basis of volume of Business

a) **Wholesale Market**: The wholesale market comes into existence when the commodities are bought and sold in bulk or large quantities.

b) **Retail Market**: When the commodities are sold in the small quantities, it is called retail market. This is the market for ultimate consumers.

On the basis of Competitions:

Based on the type of competition markets are classified into a. perfectly competitive market and b. Imperfect market. We shall study these markets in greater details in the following paragraphs.

6.1 Introduction

Efficiency of management lies in its capacity to analyze the market. Study of demand and supply, its determinants, elasticity of demand and supply, market equilibrium, basic concepts of production function, revenue analysis, pricing policies and pricing methods help in analyzing the market in a more pragmatic manner. Knowledge of market structure and different kinds of markets is of utmost importance to a business manager in taking right decision and planning business activities efficiently.

Market in economics does not refer to a place or places but to a commodity and also to buyers and sellers of that commodity who are in competition with one another e.g., the cotton market may not be confined to a particular place, but may cover the entire country and, in fact, even the entire world. Buyers and sellers of cotton may be spread all over the world.

Market situation varies in their structure. Market structure refers to economically significant features of a market, which affect the behavior, and working of firms in the industry. It tells us how a market is built up and what its basic features are. According to Pappas and Hirschey, "Market structure refers to the number and size distribution of buyers and sellers in the market for a good or service". **It indicates a set of market characteristics that determine the nature of market in which a firm operates**. Different market structures affect the behavior of sellers and buyers in different manners.

The chief characteristics are as follows –

1. The number and size distribution of sellers

A market may consist of a large, very large or a few sellers. There may be a few big firms with huge investments or a large number of small firms with limited investments. Thus, the operating size of the firm may be large or small in a market. The number and size of sellers influence the working of a market.

2. The number and size distribution of buyers

In a market, there may be large number of buyers. Similarly, a market may consist of many small buyers or only a few buyers. The total number of buyers exercises their influence on the nature of transactions in the market

3. Product differentiation

Products sold in the market may be homogeneous, or have substitutes, close substitutes or remote substitutes. A firm may deliberately differentiate its product with that of the products of other firms by adopting several techniques.

4. Condition of entry and exit

In case of a few market situations, new firms may enter the industry or old firms may leave the industry at their own free will and wish. In case of other markets, there will be deliberate entry barriers.

Thus, the characteristics of market structure give us information about the nature of working of different markets.

Thus in common parlance, market refers to a place where sellers and buyers meet for the purpose of exchanges of goods, but in the language of economics it has a wider meaning. It refers to a wide range of area where the buyers and sellers come into close contact with one another for the settlement of their transactions.

According to Prof.Cournot, the term market is "not any particular market place in which things are brought or sold, but the whole of any region in which buyers and sellers are in such free intercourse with one another that the price of the same goods tend to equality easily and quickly". In the words of Prof. Benham, Market is "any area over which buyers and sellers are in such close

Chapter 7

Market Structure

Reading Objectives:

After reading this lesson the reader will understand that the economist meaning of market is something different from the common understanding of the market. In economics, the market is the study about the demand for and supply of a particular commodity and its consequent fixing of prices for instance the market may be a bullion market, stock market, or even food grains market. The market is broadly divided into two categories like perfect market and imperfect market. The perfect market is further divided into pure market (which is a myth) and perfect market. The imperfect market is divided into monopoly market, monopolistic market, oligopoly market and duopoly market. Based on the nature of competition and on the number of buyers and sellers operating in the market, the price for the commodity may be settled at the point where the demand forces and supply forces agree upon.

Lesson Outline:

- Types of market
- Perfect market
- Pricing under perfect market
- Shutdown point
- Monopoly market

- Profit maximization under monopoly market
- Monopolistic competition
- Oligopoly market
- Kinked demand curve
- Price discrimination
- Review questions

7.1 Introduction

Market is a place where people can buy and sell commodities. It may be vegetables market, fish market, financial markets or foreign exchange markets. In economic language market is a study about the demand for and supply of a particular item and its consequent fixing of prices, example bullion on market and foreign exchange market or a commodity market like food grains market etc. Market is classified into various types based on the characteristic features. They are classified on the basis of:

Area: family market, local, regional, national and international

Time: very short period, short period, long period, very long period

Commodity: produce exchange, bullion market, capital market, stock market

Nature of Transaction: spot market, forward market and futures market

Volume of business: whole sale market, retail market

Importance: primary market, secondary market, territory market

Regulation: regulated market, unregulated market

Economics: Perfect market and imperfect market

Market In Economic Sense Implies:

1. Presence of buyers and sellers of the commodity
2. Establishment of contact between the buyer and seller
3. Similarity of the product

4. Exchange of commodity for a price

Classification Of Market Structure Based On The Nature Of Competitor:

1. Perfect market
2. Imperfect market

The imperfect market in turn can be classified as

- Monopoly market
- Duopoly market
- Oligopoly market
- Monopolistic market/ competition

The number and relative size of firms producing a good vary across industries. Market structures range from perfect competition to monopoly. Most real-world firms are along the continuum of imperfect competition. Market structure affects market outcomes, ie., the price and quantity of goods supplied.

Imperfect Competition

Perfect Competition   Monopolistic Competition   Oligopoly   Duopoly Monopoly

The above chart tells us that there are four types of imperfect competition existing in the present market environment. It is classified based on the number of buyers, sellers and competitors in the market. This chapter explains the price determination and profit maximization methods followed in these markets. Let us understand the meaning of each competition.

Monopoly market: a market with only one seller and a large number of buyers.

Monopolistic competition: a market in which firms can enter freely, each producing its own brand or version of a differentiated product.

Oligopoly market: market in which only a few firms compete with one another and entry by new firms is impeded/restricted.

Duopoly: market in which two firms compete with each other.

Monopsony: is a market with only one buyer, and a few/large sellers.

Perfect Market

Perfect competition is a market structure characterized by a complete absence of rivalry among the individual firms. A perfectly competitive firm is one whose output is so small in relation to market volume that its output decisions have no perceptible impact on price. No single producer or consumer can have control over the price or quantity of the product.

Characteristic features of perfect market:

1. Large number of buyers and sellers
2. Homogeneous product
3. Perfect knowledge about the market
4. Ruling prices
5. Absence of transport cost
6. Perfect mobility of factors
7. Profit maximization
8. Freedom in decision making

In perfect market, the price of the commodity is determined based on the demand for and supply of the product in the market. The equilibrium price and output determination is as shown in the graph.

Graph - Price And Output Determination In The Perfect Market

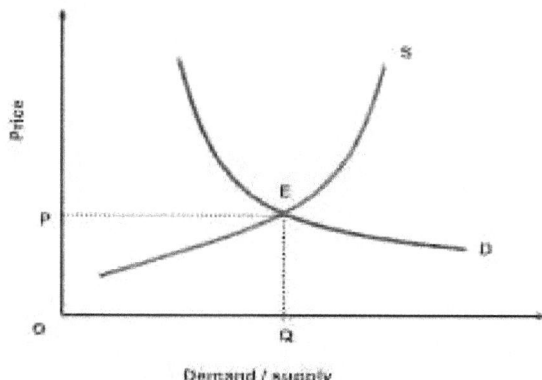

The demand curve (D) and the supply curve (S) intersect each other at a particular point which is called the equilibrium point. At the equilibrium point 'E' the quantity demanded and the quantity supplied are equal (that is OQ quantity of commodity is demanded and the same level is supplied etc). Based on the equilibrium the price of the commodity is fixed as OP. This is the fundamental pricing strategy followed in the perfect market.

Pricing Under Perfect Competition

Demand and supply curves can be used to analyze the equilibrium market price and the optimum output.

1. If quantity demanded is equal to quantity supplied at a particular price then the market is in equilibrium

2. If quantity demanded is more than the quantity supplied then market price may not be stable. i.e., it will rise.

3. If quantity demanded is less than quantity supplied then market price is fixed not in a equilibrium position.

When the price at which quantity demanded is equal to quantity supplied, buyers as well as sellers are satisfied. If price is greater than the equilibrium price, some sellers would not be able to sell the commodity. So they would try to dispose the unsold stock at a lower price. Thus the price will go on declining till they get equalized (Qd = Qs). The various possible changes in

Demand and supply are expressed in the following graphs to understand the price fluctuations in the market.

When the firm is producing its goods at the maximum level, the unit cost of production or managerial cost of the last item produced is the lowest. If the firm produces more than this, the managerial cost will rise. If that firm produces less than that level of output, it is not taking advantage of the economics of the large scale operation. When the firm produces largest level of output and sell at the managerial cost, it is said to be in equilibrium position. There is no temptation to produce more or produce less level of output. Likewise, when all the firms put together or the industry produces the largest amount of output at the lowest marginal cost, the industry is also said to be in the equilibrium

Let us assume that the demand equal to supply Qd = Qs and the equilibrium point 'E' determines the price as OP. In the short run the demand for the commodity increases but the supply remains the same. Then the demand curve shifts to the right and the new demand curve D1D1 is derived. The demand has increased from OM quantity to OM1. The new demand curve intersects the supply curve at the new equilibrium point 'E1' and the price of the commodity is increased from OP to OP1. Therefore it is clear that when demand increases without any change in supply this leads to price rise in the market.

Graph – Price And Quantity Variability When Increase In Demand

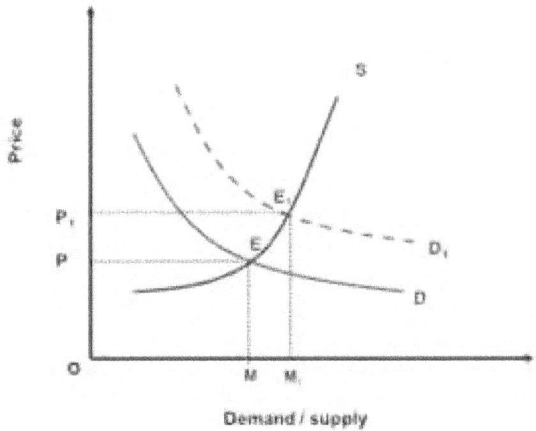

If the demand remains the same and the firm tries to supply more of the commodity, then the supply curve shifts from SS to S1S1 (Graph - below). Earlier the equilibrium point was 'E' and the price of the commodity was OP. Due to change in supply the equilibrium point has changed into 'E1' which in turn reduced the price form OP to OP0. Therefore if the firm supplies more than the demand this leads to price fall in the market.

Graph – Price And Quantity Variability When Increase In Price

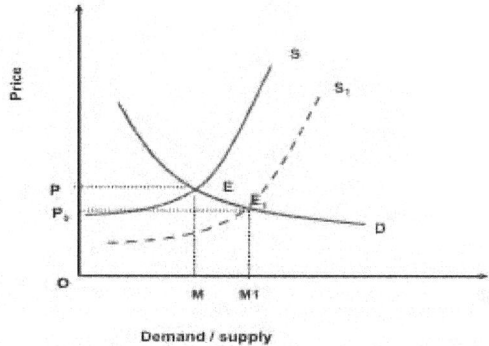

If the firm changes its supply due to increase in demand then the possible fluctuations in the price is explained below. Let us assume that the firm increased its supply 10%, the demand has also increased but not in the same proportion – it increased only 2% ($\Delta Qd < \Delta Qs$). From the graph we can understand that the equilibrium point 'E' has changed into 'E1' which reduced the price of the commodity from OP to OP1.

Graph – Price And Variability When Change In Demand Is Less Than Change In Supply

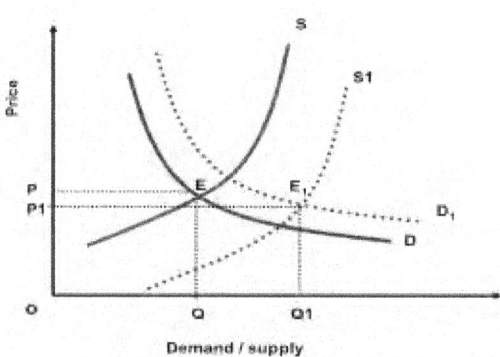

On the other hand when there is 10% increase in the demand and the supply has increased only to 2%, the new demand curve D1D1 and the new supply curve S1S1 intersect each other at the new equilibrium point 'E1'.

The price of the commodity is OP at 'E' and it increases from P to P1 and becomes OP1.i.e. When the demand increases more than the supply (ΔQd > ΔQs) the price of the commodity will increase.

Graph – Price And Quantity Variability When Change In Demand Is More Than The Change In Supply

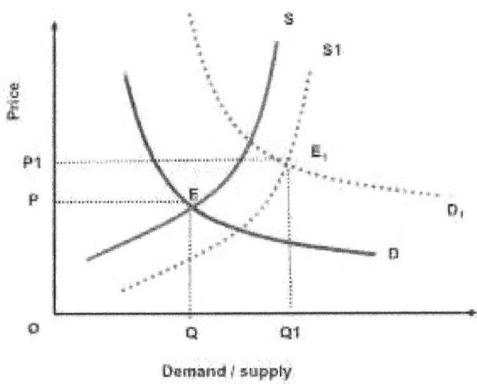

The following graph explains clearly that both the demand for the commodity and the supply increases in the same proportion (i.e. ΔQD = ΔQS).The shift in supply curve and the shift in demand curve are in the same level and the new equilibrium point 'E1' determines the same price OP level. There is no change in the price when the demand and supply are equal.

Graph – Price And Quantity Variabilty When Change In Demand And Supply Equally

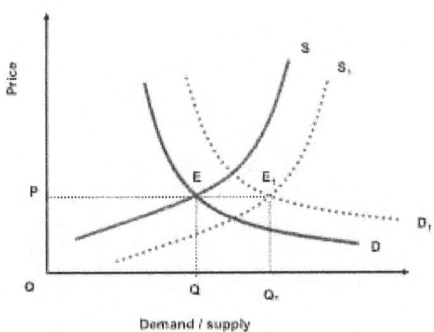

Profit Maximization Under Perfect Competition

The primary objective of any business is to maximize the profit. Profit can be increased either by increasing total revenue (TR) or by reducing the total cost (TC). The profit is nothing but the difference between the revenue and the cost.

The total profit = TR – TC

Let us assume that whatever produced is sold in the market.

TR = Quantity sold   x   price

To increase the revenue, it is better to either increase the quantity sold or increase the price. Therefore while increasing the revenue or minimizing the total cost of production over a period of time with attendant economies of scale will widen the difference to gain more profit.

In perfect market, the firm's Marginal cost, Average cost, Average revenue, Marginal revenue are equal to the price of the commodity. The cost is measured as average cost and marginal cost .When the firm is in equilibrium, producing the maximum output i.e. cost of the last item produced is known as marginal cost.The total cost divided by the number of goods produced will give the average cost. When the firm is operating in perfect market MC = AC.

In the same way the revenue available to the firm through selling goods is called as total revenue.The last item sold is the marginal revenue. The total revenue divided by the number of items sold is the average revenue and when the firm is working in the perfect market the MR shall be equal to AR. Therefore the MC = MR = AR = AC = P in the short run. The size of the plant is fixed only with the variable factors and the price is fixed by the demand and supply.

Perfect Market Price Determination Graph (a) Graph (b)

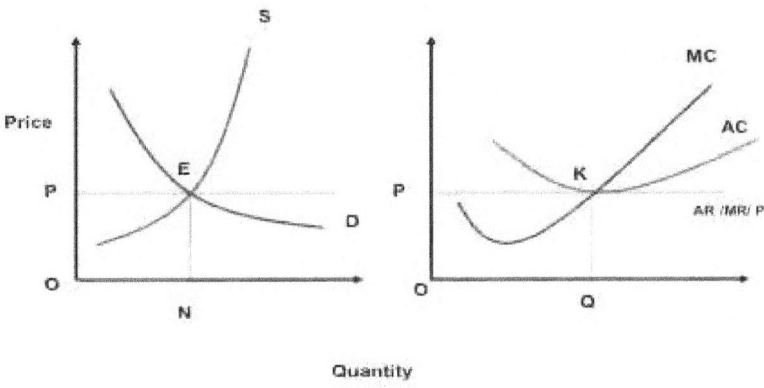

Quantity

The demand for the commodity is expressed in the demand curve (D) and the supply (S) curve is known as S curve. The point of intersection of the D curve and S Curve is the equilibrium point (E) where the price is determined as OP. (Rs.10) The average revenue per unit is also Rs.10 expressed in graph (b) along with the marginal cost (MC) and average cost (AC) curves. The MC and AC intersect at point 'K' which is equal to the price OP / AR / MR. Therefore we can say that P=AR=AC=MR=MC at this level. At this equilibrium point buyers and sellers are satisfied with their price. The price of the commodity includes the normal profit through the average cost. The average cost consists of implicit and explicit costs. That means the organizers knowledge, time, idea and effort is also considered in the cost of production. Let us assume that in the short run the demand for the commodity increases, then the change in price and profit are explained in the graph below.

Graph - Short Run Profit Maximization Under Perfect Competition

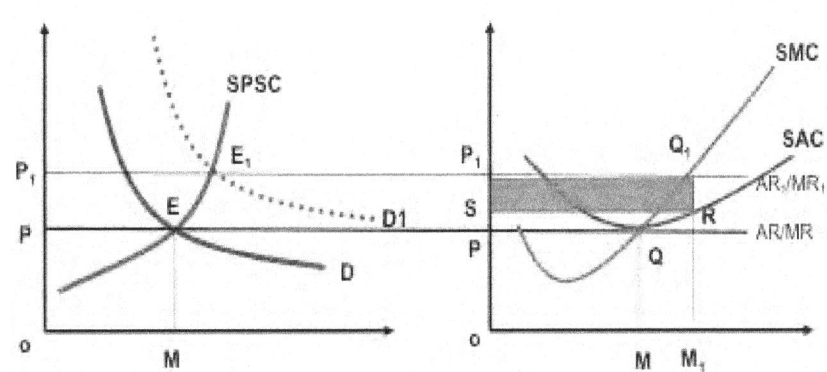

From the above graph we can understand that in the short run demand curve DD and the short period supply curve SPSC intersects at 'E' and the price of the commodity is determined as OP. The right side graph indicates the cost and revenue curves. The average revenue (AR) and marginal revenue (MR) are equal to the price of the commodity OP. The short period marginal cost (SMC) and short period average cost (SAC) are also depicted in the graph. The minimum average cost is selected based on the equilibrium point Q which produces optimum quantity of OM. The marginal cost curve and average cost curve intersects at the point Q that means QM amount (rupees) is spent as marginal as well as average cost. The SAC is tangential to AR/MR at this point therefore we can conclude that the price of the commodity is equal to the average cost, average revenue, marginal cost and marginal revenue (P = AR = MR = AC = MC)

If the demand increases in the market then the new demand curve D1D1 intersects the SPSC at the new equilibrium point 'E1' and the price increases from OP to OP1. Therefore the average revenue also increases from AR to AR1. At this situation P1 = AR1 = MR1 but the SMC curve intersects at Q1 ie., new equilibrium point and the OM quantity has increased from OM to OM1 in the 'X' axis. The average cost has increased as M1R.

The profit = Total Revenue (TR) – Total Cost (TC) TR = quantity sold x price

TC = average cost x quantity produced

TR = OM1 x OP1 = OM1Q1P1 TC = M1R x OM1 = OM1RS

Profit = OM1Q1P1 − OM1RS = P1Q1RS

In the above graph, the shaded portion of P1Q1RS is the total profit earned by the firm in the short run but in the long run the organization

will increase the production and will supply more of the commodity. Ultimately both the demand and the supply gets equalized and the short run abnormal profit becomes normal. Therefore we can conclude that even in the perfect market it is possible to earn profit in the short period.

It indicates clearly that in the short run, in any perfect market, the increase in demand will increase the profit to the businessmen. The normal profit will be there until it gets equalized with the demand i.e. new D1D1 with the increased supply of S1S1.

This economic profit attracts new firms into the industry and the entry of these new firms increases the industry supply. This increased supply pushes down the price. As price falls, all firms in the industry adjust their output levels in order to remain in profit maximizing equilibrium. New firms continue to enter the industry and price continues to fall, and existing firms continue to adjust their outputs until all economic profits are eliminated. There is no longer an incentive for the new firms to enter and the owners of all firms in the industry will earn only what they could make through their best alternatives.

Economic losses motivate some to exit (shut down) from the industry. The exit of these firms decreases industry supply. The reduction in supply pushes up market price and all the firms shall adjust their output in order to maximize their profit.

Shut Down Point:

If the market price for the product is below minimum average variable cost, the firm will cease to produce, if this appears to be not just a temporary phenomenon. When the price is less than average variable cost it will neither cover fixed cost nor a part of the variable costs. Then the firm can minimize losses up to total fixed costs only by not producing. It is therefore regarded as the shut down point.

In the short run, a firm can be in equilibrium at various levels depending upon different cost and market price conditions. But these are temporary equilibrium points. Thus at this unstable equilibrium point the firm gets excess profits or normal profit and sometimes incur loss also.

Consequences Of Pure Competition

Perfect competition ensures maximum welfare of the people as a whole. Each firm tends to attain the most efficient size to expand output and to reduce the average cost of production.

Lessons For Managers

1. Important to enter a growing market as far ahead of the competitors as possible. When there is fall in supply and increase in prices, take advantage before the new entrants.

2. Due to profit new entrants are willing to offer ,low priced therefore a firm should be among the lowest cost producer to ensure its survival.

3. Differentiation offers temporary relief for competition pressure.

4. Due to globalization firms enjoy advantage of cheap labour and disadvantage of technology up gradation.

Review Questions:

1. Define the market and market structure.
2. Explain various types of markets with suitable examples.
3. Distinguish between perfect and imperfect market.
4. List out the major characteristic features of a perfect market.
5. Show graphically how an individual firm attains equilibrium under perfect competition.
6. Explain how the price and output is determined in perfect competition.
7. Is it possible to earn profit in the perfect competition? Justify.
8. What do you mean by shut down point? Explain why a firm suffering from losses.

Exercise:

How will each of the following changes in demand and supply affect equilibrium price and equilibrium price and equilibrium quantity in a competitive market; that is, do price and quantity rise, fall or remain unchanged or are the answers indeterminate because they depend on the magnitude of the shift. Use supply and demand diagrams to verify your answers.

a) Supply increases and Demand is constant

b) Demand increases and Supply is constant

c) Supply increases and Demand is constant

d) Demand increases and Supply increases

e) Demand increases and Supply is constant

f) Supply increases and Demand increases

g) Demand increase and Supply decreases

h) Demand decreases and Supply decreases

Monopoly Market

Mono means single, poly means seller and hence monopoly is a market structure where only one sells the goods and many buyers buy the same. Monopoly lies at the opposite extreme from perfect competition on the market structure continuum. A firm produces the entire supply of a particular good or service that has no close substitute.

Characteristic Features:

1. A single seller in the market
2. There are no close substitutes
3. There is a restriction for the entry and exit for the firms in the market
4. Imperfect dissemination of information

This does not mean that the monopoly firms are large in size. For example a doctor who has a clinic in a village has no other competitor in the village but in the town there may be more doctors. Therefore the barrier to the entry is due to economies of scale, economies of scope, cost complementarities, patents and other legal barriers.

Profit maximization under Monopoly Competition

For monopolist there are two options for maximizing the profit i.e. maximize the output and the limit the price or limit the production of the goods and services and fix a higher price (market driven price). In monopoly competition, the demand curve of the firm is identical to the market demand curve of that product. In monopoly the MR is always less than the price of the commodity.

Profit Maximization Rule:

Produce at that rate of output where MR = MC. From the graph we can understand the profit maximization under monopoly. 'X' axis indicates the output and 'Y' the price/cost and revenue. The marginal revenue curve is denoted as MR. The average revenue curve is AR which is also the demand curve. MC is the marginal cost curve, It looks like a tick mark and average cost curve AC is boat shape.

Graph- Profit Maximization Under Monopoly Market

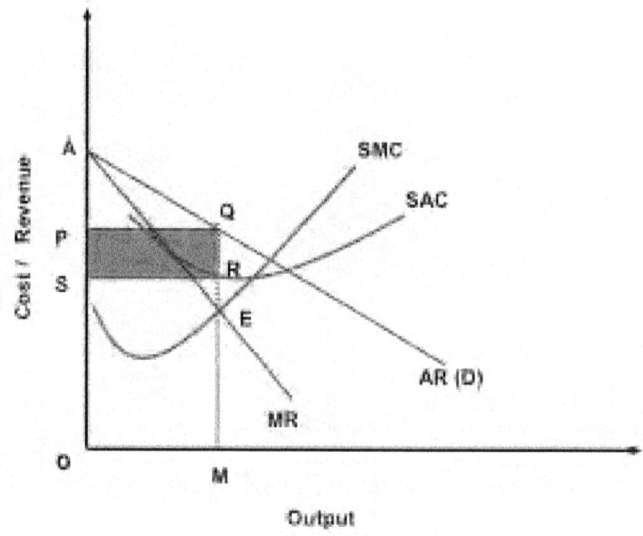

From the above graph it is seen that the demand curve D and average revenue curve AR are depicted as a single curve. The marginal revenue curve MR also slopes the same but the MR curve is below the AR curve. The short run marginal cost curve SMC looks like a tick mark and the boat shaped average cost curve SAC is also seen in the graph. The profit maximization criteria of MR=MC is followed in the monopoly market and the equilibrium point 'E' is derived from the intersection of

MR and SMC curves in the short run. i.e. MC curve or SMC here intersects the MR curve from below. Based on the equilibrium point, the output is the optimum level of production i.e., at OM quantity. The price of the commodity is determined as OP. On an average the firm receives MQ amount as revenue. The total revenue of selling OM quantity gives OMQP amount of total revenue (OM quantity x OP price). The firm has spent MR as an average cost to produce OM quantity and the total cost of production is OMRS (OM quantity x MR cost per unit)

Profit	=	TR - TC
	=	OMQP - OMRS
	=	PQRS (the shaded portion in the graph)

In the short run the monopoly firm will earn profit continuously even with various returns.

Graph- Monopoly Profit With Increasing Cost

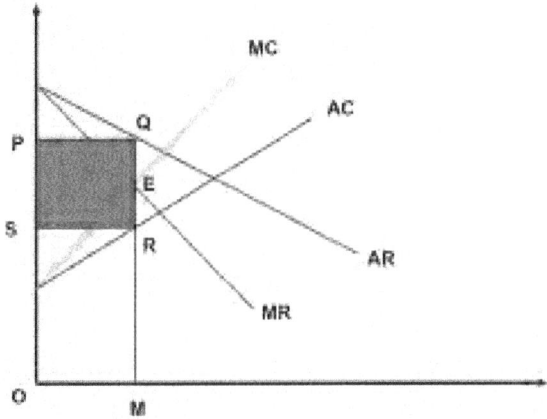

From the above graph it can be understood that the cost of production (MC, AC) is increasing along with the output but even with the increasing scale the firm earns PQRS as profit which is the shaded portion in the graph.

The graph given below explains clearly that the firms cost curves of Marginal cost (MC) and Average cost (AC) are declining with this slope. The organization earns PQRS profit but the profit is comparatively lesser than the previous situation.

Graph – Monopoly Profit Under Decreasing Cost

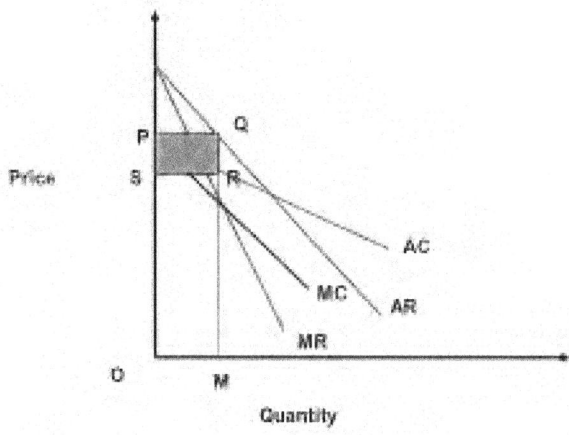

The third situation explains that the organizations' marginal cost and average cost curves are horizontal and parallel to the X axis. Even with the constant scale, the firms earns profit as PQRS.

Graph – Monopoly Profit Under Constant Cost

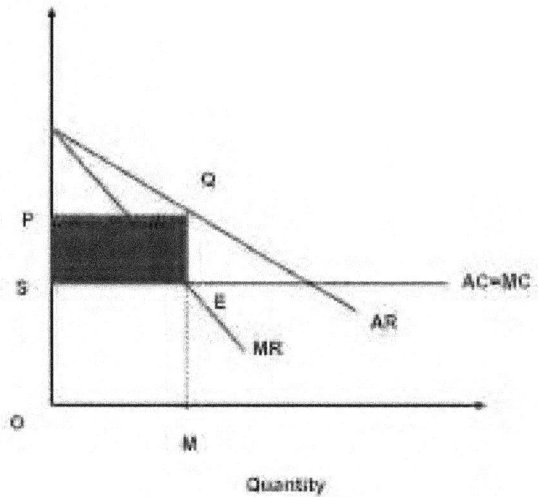

Therefore we can conclude by saying that under monopoly market structure the firm will earn profit even under different cost conditions and profit maximization takes place. They follow the price determination condition as MC=MR and never incur loss.

Difference Between Perfect And Monopoly Market:

1. Perfect market is unrealistic in practical life. But slowly certain commodities are moving towards it. Monopoly market exists in real time.

2. Under perfect market only homogenous products are sold but on the other hand monopoly market deals with different products.

3. Under perfect competition, price is determined by demand and supply of the market. But in monopoly the seller determines the price of the good.

4. Monopolist can control the market price but in perfect competition the sellers have no control over the market price.

5. There is no advertisement cost in perfect market. In other markets it is essential and it is included in the cost of production and is reflected in the price.

6. Monopolist sell their products higher than the perfect competitors except when there is government regulation or adverse public opinion.

Lessons For Managers:

1. The seller has to fix the price based on the marginal revenue and marginal cost instead of focusing on their profit.

2. It is essential to understand the substitutes and their market competition.

3. Under monopoly for certain products buyer has more market power.

4. Government policies can also change at any time.

5. Monopolist in domestic market may face tough competition from imported products.

Review Questions:

1. Mention the characteristic features of Monopoly market.
2. Distinguish between monopoly and perfect market.
3. Describe graphically the pricing and profit determination under monopoly market.
4. A monopolist aims at maximizing price rather than profits, do you agree with this statement?

Monopolistic Competition

The perfect competition and monopoly are the two extreme forms. To bridge the gap the concept of monopolistic competition was developed by Edward Chamberlin. It has both the elements like many small sellers and many small buyers. There is product differentiation. Therefore close substitutes are available and at the same time it is easy to enter and easy to exit from the market. Therefore it is possible to incur loss in this market. The profit maximization for each firm, for each product depends upon the differentiation and advertising expenditure. As every firm is acting as a monopoly the same logic of monopoly is followed. Each and every firm will have their own set of cost and revenue curves and the price determination is based on the rule of MR=MC and they incur varied profits according to their market structure. But in the monopolistic competition number of monopoly competitors will be there in different levels. They monopolize in a small geographical area or a segment or a model.

The demand curve of a monopolistically competitive firm would be more elastic than that of a purely monopolistic firm. The cost function of a firm would be that there will not be any significant difference across different types of structures in the product market. Given the function, and the corresponding AR and MR curves, and the cost function, and the corresponding SAC and SMC curves, the price and output determination of a profit – maximizing monopolistically competitive firm could be as follows.

Graph – Pricing Under Monopolistic Competition With Profit

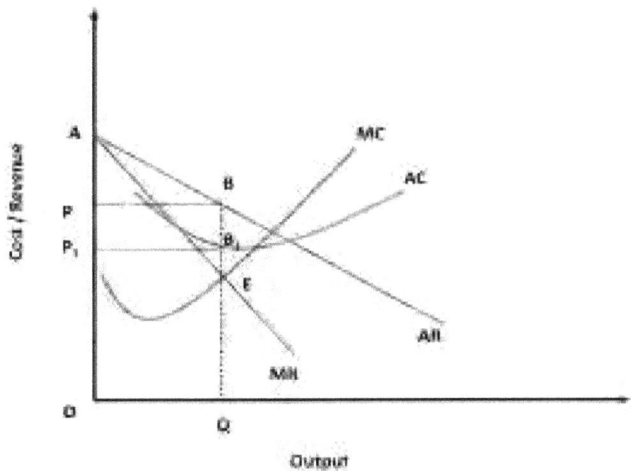

From the above graph we can understand that under monopolistic competition firms incur profit which is PP1BB1 the pricing and profit

determination are similar to the monopoly market. MR is marginal

revenue curve AR is average revenue and demand curve. At point 'E' both MR and marginal cost curve MC intersects. Based on this equilibrium the product is sold at OP price in the market. The Average cost curve indicates that the firm has spent QB1 amount per unit but it receives QB through its sale. Therefore the difference between the two BB1 is the profit margin which should be multiplied with the total quantity sold OQ which gives PP1BB1 amount of profit.

Graph – Pricing under Monopolistic competition with loss

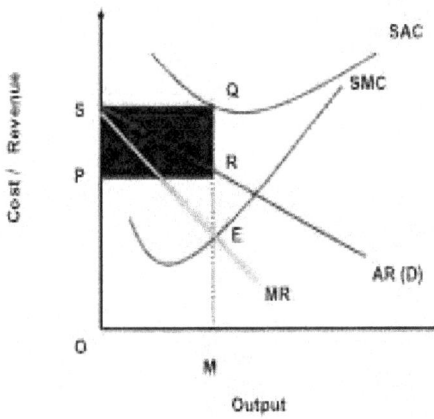

The marginal revenue curve MR and the average revenue curve AR that is the demand curve is also represented in the graph. The condition for product decision is MR=MC. The MR and MC intersect at point 'E' based on the equilibrium. It is decided to produce OM quantity and the price of the commodity is fixed at OP in the market. Therefore the total revenue by selling OM quantity in the market for OP price is equal to OM x OP = OPRM. But to produce OM quantity the firm has spent MQ as average cost. Therefore the total cost of production = OM x MQ = OMQS.

Therefore the profit = TR – TC

= ORPM – OMQS

= - PQRS. (Negative)

That means the cost of production per unit is more than the average revenue earned per unit. Average revenue = MR and the Average cost = MQ which is more than the revenue. Therefore the difference QR is the loss per unit multiplied with OM quantity. PQRS is the total loss to the organization.

Lessons For Managers:

1. A firm must concentrate on differentiation and building brand value.
2. The managers must never be complacent with their profit because of new entrants.
3. The market is competing with differentiated products at lowest price.
4. Need not offer at low price always. Through supplying best products he can retain his price and profit.

Oligopoly Market

This is a market consisting of a few firms relatively large firms, each with a substantial share of the market and all recognizing their interdependence. It is a common form of market structure. The products may be identical or differentiated. The price determination and profit maximization is based on how the competitors will respond to price or output changes.

There Are Different **Types Of Oligopoly:**

1. <u>Pure and perfect oligopoly</u> : if the firm produced homogeneous products it is perfect oligopoly. If there is product differentiation then it is called as imperfect or differentiated oligopoly.

2. <u>Open and closed oligopoly</u> : entry is not possible. When it is closed to the new entrants then it is closed oligopoly. On the other hand entry is accepted in open oligopoly.

3. <u>Partial and full oligopoly</u> : under partial oligopoly industry is dominated by one large firm who is a price leader and others follow. In full oligopoly no price leadership.

4. <u>Syndicated and organized oligopoly</u> : where the firms sell their products through a centralized syndicate. On the other hand firms organize themselves into a central association for fixing prices, output and quotas.

Characteristic Features Of An Oligopoly Market:

1. Few sellers
2. Lack of uniformity in the product
3. Advertisement cost is included
4. No monopoly competition
5. Firms struggle constantly
6. There is interdependency
7. Experience of Group behavior
8. Price rigidity
9. Price leadership
10. Barriers to entry

<u>Price rigidity</u> : the price will be kept unchanged due to fear of retaliation and prices tend to be strict and inflexible. No firm would indulge in price cutting as it would eventually lead to a price war with no benefit to anyone.

Reasons for rigidity are: firms know ultimate outcome of price cutting; large firms incur more expenditure than others; keeping the price low to reduce the new entrants; increased price rise leads to reduction in number of customers.

The oligopoly prices are indeterminate. The demand function is then an important ingredient in the price determination mechanism. Several theories of oligopoly prices have been developed and each one of them is based on a particular assumption about the reactions of the rival firms and the firms' actions. The popular models and appropriate classifications are discussed below.

Oligopoly Models:

1. **Cournot oligopoly:** There are few firms producing differentiated or homogeneous products and each firm believes that competitors will hold their output constant if it changes its output.

2. **Stackelberg oligopoly:** Few firms and differentiated or homogeneous product. The leader chooses an output and others follow.

3. **Bertrand oligopoly:** Few firms produce identical product. Firms compete in price and react optimally to competitor's prices.

4. **Sweezy oligopoly:** An industry in which there are few firms serving many consumers. Firms produce differentiated products and each firm believes competitors will respond to a price reduction but they will not follow a price increase.

Kinked Demand Curve

When a firm increases its price, the rival firms do not follow it by increasing their prices in turn this increases its market share. When a firm reduces its price rival firms immediately follows it by decreasing their prices. If they do not do so, customers go to the firm which is offering at lower price. This is the fundamental behaviour of the firms in an oligopoly market. Let us understand the unique characteristic feature of kinked demand curve.

The demand curve in oligopoly has two parts. (i) relatively elastic demand curve (ii) relatively inelastic demand curve as shown in the graph below. In oligopoly market firms are reluctant to change prices even if the cost of production (or) demand changes. Price rigidity is the basis for the kinked demand curve. Each firm faces demand curve kinked at the currently prevailing price. At higher prices demand is highly elastic, whereas at lower prices it is inelastic.

Graph – Kinked Demand Curve

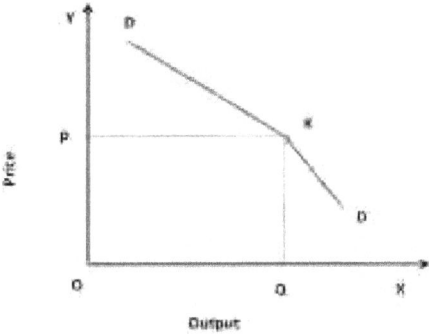

From the graph we can understand that OP is the given price. There is a kink at point K on demand curve (DD). Therefore DK is the elasticity segment and KD is the inelastic segment. There is a change in the slope of the demand curve at K. At this situation the firm follows the prevailing price and does not make any change in it because rising of price would contract sales as demand tends to be more elastic at this stage. I would also fear losing buyers due to competitor's price who have not raised their prices. On the other hand lowering of price would imply an immediate retaliation from the rivals on account of close interdependence of price, output movement in the oligopoly market. Therefore the firm will not expect much rise in sale with price reduction.

Graph – Marginal Revenue Curve In Oligopoly Market

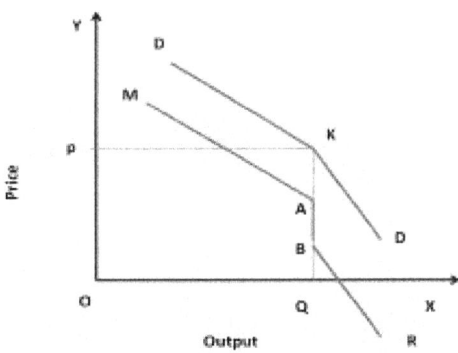

The average revenue curve and the demand curve (DD) of an oligopoly firm has a kink. The kinked average revenue curve implies a discontinuation in the marginal revenues curve. It explains the phenomenon of price rigidity in oligopoly market.

Graph – Price Rigidity Under Oligopoly Market

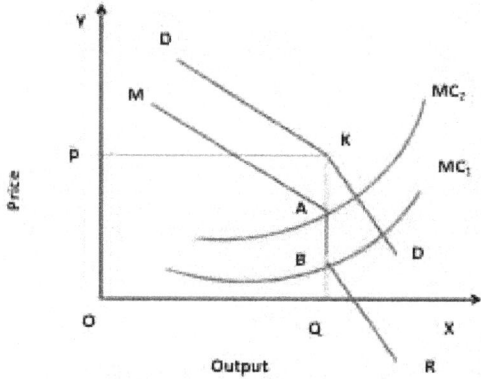

The price output level that maximizes the profits for a firm is derived from the equilibrium point, which lies at the intersection of the MC and the MR curves. The price output combination can remain optimal at the kink even though the MC fluctuates because of the associated gap in the MR curve. This is shown in the graph. The profit maximizing price OP and output combination of OQ remains unchanged as long as MC fluctuates between MC1 and MC2 that is between A and B. Hence there is price rigidity- it means OP does not change. It is concluded that once a general price level is reached it remains unchanged over a period of time in oligopoly market.

1. Managers should concentrate on their research and development to bring new products and quality of service to raise their economies of scale.

2. Due to kinked demand curve, increase in cost of production will not affect their price.

3. Product differentiation and advertisement play a major role in increasing market share.

Price Discrimination

Price discrimination means that the producer charges different prices for different consumers for the same goods and service. Price discrimination occurs when prices differ even though costs are same. For example, Doctors charge different fees for different customers. In case they charge different prices in different markets, people go to the market where price is low. Then it gets equalized in the long run. There are various **types** of price discrimination:

They are:

1. Personal Discrimination
2. Place Discrimination
3. Trade Discrimination
4. Time Discrimination
5. Age Discrimination
6. Sex Discrimination
7. Location Discrimination
8. Size Discrimination
9. Quality Discrimination
10. Special Service
11. Use of services
12. Product Discrimination

Objectives Of Price Discrimination:

1. To dispose the surpluses
2. To develop new market
3. To Maximize use of unutilized capacity
4. To Earn monopoly profit
5. To Retain export market

6. To Increase the sales

Degrees Of Price Discrimination:

First Degree Price Discrimination:

Firm charges a different price to each of its customers. The maximum willingness to pay is fixed as price which is called as reservation price. In perfect market the difference between demand and marginal revenue is the profit (for additional unit producing and selling). Firms do not know the customers willingness, therefore different prices. In imperfect market it is not possible to price for each and every customer.

Graph – First Degree Price Discrimination

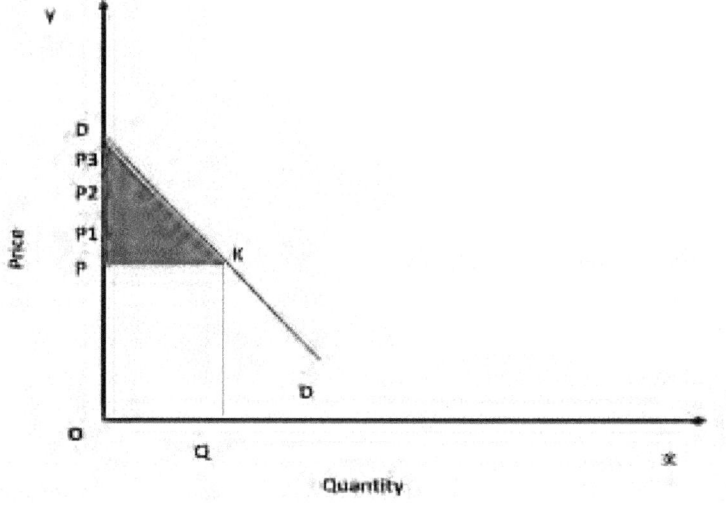

Second Degree Discrimination:

Firm charges different prices per unit for different quantities of the same goods or service. They follow block pricing method. The units in a particular block will be uniformly priced. The possible maximum price is charged for some given minimum block of output purchased by the buyers and then the additional blocks are sold at lower prices.

Graph – Second Degree Price Discrimination

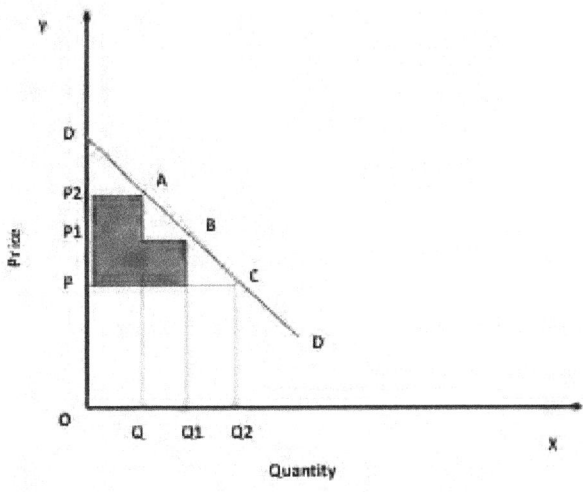

Third Degree Discrimination:

Firm segments the customers into groups with separate demand curves and charges different prices from each group.

In first degree price discrimination, in case of unit wise differing prices, the second degree price discrimination is a case of block wise differing prices. In second degree discrimination a part of consumer's surplus is captured. But the third degree is commonly used. The firm divides its total output into many submarkets and sets different prices for its product in each market in relation to the demand elasticity.

Graph – Third Degree Price Discrimination

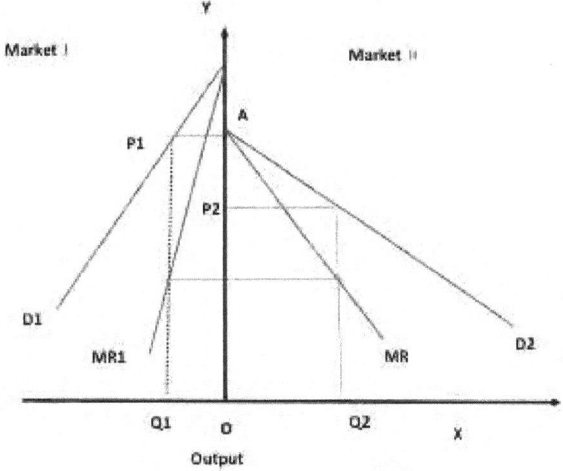

There are two markets I and II their demand curves D1 and D2 is given. D1 is less elastic and D2 is more elastic demand curve. The firm distributes OQ1 to market - I at OP1 price and OQ2 to the market II at OP2 price. Market- I has less elastic demand therefore higher price is charged.

The pricing mechanisms in different market structures provide a sound theoretical base to understand how price and output decisions are made. There are several other methods commonly followed in practice. However, price discrimination does not receive social and moral justification in the society.

Comparison Of Various Market Structure

	Perfect Market	Monopoly	Monopolistic	Oligopoly
Number of competitors	Many small buyers and sellers	Single seller	Many sellers	
Product differentiation	Homogeneous	High differentiation, no close substitutes	Differentiation among competitors	
Information	Complete and free information	Less information	Less information	Restricted access to price and product information
Conditions of entry and exit	Easy to enter and exit	High barriers due to economies of scale	Easy to enter and exit	High barriers to entry
Profit potential	Normal profit in long run, economic profit in short run	Economic profit in long run and short run	Economic profit in short run and normal in long run	Economic profit in both short and long run
Example	Agricultural products	Railways	Clothing	Automobiles

Case Studies

Case Study 1: The Housing Market

The housing market is a classic example of how supply and demand can affect prices. When there is a shortage of housing, prices tend to rise. This is because people are willing to pay more for a scarce good. When there is an excess supply of housing, prices tend to fall. This is because people have more options and are less willing to pay a high price.

In recent years, the housing market in the United States has experienced a significant increase in prices. This is due to a number of factors, including:

- A decrease in the supply of housing. This is due to a number of factors, including the aging of the population, which has led to a decrease in the number of new households being formed, and the increasing cost of construction, which has made it more difficult for builders to construct new homes.

- An increase in demand for housing. This is due to a number of factors, including the strong economy, which has led to more people being able to afford to buy homes, and the low interest rates, which have made it more affordable to borrow money to buy a home.

The increase in housing prices has been a major concern for many people, especially those who are trying to buy their first home. However, it is important to remember that the housing market is cyclical and that prices are likely to eventually come down.

Here are some other factors that can affect the supply and demand for housing:

- Changes in interest rates. When interest rates are low, it is more affordable to borrow money to buy a home, which can lead to an increase in demand. When interest rates are high, it is less affordable to borrow money, which can lead to a decrease in demand.

- Changes in the economy. When the economy is strong, more people are able to afford to buy homes, which can lead to an increase in demand. When the economy is weak, fewer people are able to afford to buy homes, which can lead to a decrease in demand.

- Changes in government regulations. Government regulations can affect the supply and demand for housing in a number of ways. For example, zoning laws can restrict the amount of housing that can be built in a particular area, which can lead to a decrease in supply.

The law of supply and demand is a powerful force that affects the prices of goods and services in many different markets. By understanding how supply and demand work, we can better understand the factors that influence prices and make informed decisions about our spending

Case Study2: The Price Rise of FMCG Products in India

The price of fast-moving consumer goods (FMCG) products in India has been rising steadily in recent months. This is due to a number of factors, including:

- Inflation: The overall inflation rate in India has been rising, and this has put upward pressure on the prices of all goods and services, including FMCG products.

- Increase in input costs: The cost of raw materials, packaging, and transportation has been rising, which has also contributed to the price rise of FMCG products.

- Weaker rupee: The depreciation of the Indian rupee against the US dollar has made imported raw materials and packaging more expensive, which has also pushed up the prices of FMCG products.

- Competition: The FMCG market in India is highly competitive, and companies are constantly trying to differentiate their products and attract customers. This has led to some companies cutting costs, which can lead to lower quality products and/or higher prices.

The price rise of FMCG products has been a major concern for many consumers in India. This is especially true for lower-income households, who spend a large portion of their income on these products. The price rise has also put pressure on the margins of FMCG companies.

There are a number of factors that could potentially slow down or reverse the price rise of FMCG products in India. These include:

- A slowdown in inflation: If the overall inflation rate in India slows down, it will put downward pressure on the prices of all goods and services, including FMCG products.

- A decrease in input costs: If the cost of raw materials, packaging, and transportation decreases, it will also help to lower the prices of FMCG products.

- A stronger rupee: If the Indian rupee strengthens against the US dollar, it will make imported raw materials and packaging cheaper, which will also help to lower the prices of FMCG products.

- Less competition: If the FMCG market in India becomes less competitive, companies may be less likely to cut costs, which could help to keep prices down.

The price rise of FMCG products is a complex issue with no easy solutions. However, by understanding the factors that are driving the price rise, we can better understand how to address it.

In addition to the factors mentioned above, there are a few other things that can be done to help address the price rise of FMCG products in India. These include:

- Government intervention: The government could intervene to regulate the prices of FMCG products. This could be done by imposing price controls or by providing subsidies to FMCG companies.

- Promoting competition: The government could promote competition in the FMCG market by removing barriers to entry for new companies. This would help to keep prices down.

- Educating consumers: Consumers can be educated about the factors that are driving the price rise of FMCG products. This can help them to make informed decisions about their spending and to demand lower prices from companies.

The price rise of FMCG products is a significant challenge facing consumers and businesses in India. However, by taking steps to address the underlying factors, we can help to mitigate the impact of this price rise.

Case Study3: The Consumer Surplus from Free Wi-Fi

Many businesses offer free Wi-Fi to their customers. This is done in order to attract customers, to make it easier for customers to do business with them, and to improve the customer experience.

The consumer surplus from free Wi-Fi is the difference between the amount that consumers are willing to pay for Wi-Fi and the amount that they actually pay, which is zero. For example, let's say that you are willing to pay $10 per hour to use free Wi-Fi at a coffee shop. The consumer surplus from the free Wi-Fi is $10, which is the amount of money you save by not having to pay for it.

The consumer surplus from free Wi-Fi can be significant. A study by the Pew Research Center found that 72% of Americans use free Wi-Fi at least once a week. The study also found that the average American saves $100 per year by using free Wi-Fi.

The consumer surplus from free Wi-Fi is a benefit to consumers. It allows them to save money and to enjoy a better customer experience. Businesses that offer free Wi-Fi can attract more customers and improve their bottom line.

Here are some other examples of consumer surplus:

- The consumer surplus from a sale. When a product is on sale, consumers are able to buy it for less than they are willing to pay. This creates consumer surplus.

- The consumer surplus from a new product. When a new product is introduced, consumers are often willing to pay a premium for it. This creates consumer surplus.

- The consumer surplus from a government subsidy. When the government subsidizes a good or service, it lowers the price for consumers. This creates consumer surplus.

Consumer surplus is an important concept in economics. It measures the benefit that consumers receive from a product or service. Consumer surplus can be used to evaluate government policies and to make decisions about the allocation of resources.

Case Study4: 1991 Economic reforms in India

The economic reforms of 1991 were a series of policy changes implemented by the Government of India in response to a severe balance of payments crisis. The reforms were designed to liberalize the Indian economy and make it more attractive to foreign investment.

Key reforms

The key reforms of 1991 included:

- Deregulation of the industrial sector: The government abolished industrial licensing and allowed private sector companies to enter new industries.

- Reduction of import tariffs: The government lowered import tariffs on capital goods and raw materials.

- Liberalization of foreign investment: The government allowed foreign companies to invest in India without prior government approval.

- Reform of the financial sector: The government deregulated the banking sector and allowed foreign banks to operate in India.

Impact Of The Reforms

The economic reforms of 1991 had a significant impact on the Indian economy. The reforms led to a surge in foreign investment, which helped to boost economic growth. The reforms also led to increased competition in the Indian market, which benefited consumers.

The following are some of the key benefits of the economic reforms of 1991:

- Increased economic growth: The Indian economy grew at an average rate of 7% per year between 1991 and 2008.

- Reduced poverty: The poverty rate in India fell from 45% in 1991 to 22% in 2011.

- Increased employment: The number of jobs in India increased by 50% between 1991 and 2008.

- Improved standard of living: The average Indian's standard of living improved significantly between 1991 and 2008.

Challenges

The economic reforms of 1991 also faced some challenges. Some of the key challenges included:

- Increased inequality: The reforms led to increased inequality in India, as the benefits of economic growth were not evenly distributed.

- Environmental degradation: The reforms led to increased environmental degradation, as industries were allowed to pollute without proper regulation.

- Corruption: The reforms also led to increased corruption, as government officials were able to take advantage of the new economic opportunities.

Overall impact

Despite the challenges, the economic reforms of 1991 had a positive overall impact on the Indian economy. The reforms helped to boost economic growth, reduce poverty, and improve the standard of living for millions of Indians.

The economic reforms of 1991 are considered to be one of the most significant events in Indian history. The reforms helped to transform India from a closed, inward-looking economy to a more open and globalized economy. The reforms also helped to lay the foundation for the sustained economic growth that India has experienced in recent decades.

Case study5: Freebies by Government

The practice of providing government freebies has been a long-standing tradition in India. Freebies can take many forms, including cash transfers, food subsidies, free healthcare, and free education.

Arguments in favor of government freebies There are a number of arguments in favor of government freebies. Some of these arguments include:

- Freebies can help to reduce poverty and inequality.
- Freebies can improve the quality of life for the poor and marginalized.
- Freebies can stimulate the economy by increasing demand for goods and services.
- Freebies can help to build political support for the government.

Arguments against government freebies

There are also a number of arguments against government freebies. Some of these arguments include:

- Freebies can be expensive and can lead to a fiscal burden.
- Freebies can discourage people from working and can create a culture of dependency.
- Freebies can distort the market and can lead to inefficient allocation of resources.
- Freebies can be used to buy votes and can undermine the democratic process.

Impact of government freebies in India

The impact of government freebies in India is a complex issue. There is no doubt that freebies have helped to reduce poverty and improve the quality of life for many Indians. However, there is also evidence that freebies have led to a fiscal burden, discouraged people from working, and distorted the market.

The debate over government freebies is likely to continue in India. There is no easy answer to the question of whether freebies are good or bad. The answer likely depends on the specific circumstances and the way in which freebies are implemented.

Conclusion

Government freebies are a double-edged sword. They can have both positive and negative impacts. The decision of whether or not to provide government freebies is a complex one that should be made on a case-by-case basis.

Case Study6: The Willingness of Consumers to Pay for Organic Food

Organic food is food that is produced using methods that do not involve the use of synthetic pesticides, herbicides, or fertilizers. Organic food is often perceived as being healthier and more environmentally friendly than conventional food.

There are a number of factors that can influence the willingness of consumers to pay for organic food. These factors include:

- Perceptions of health: Consumers who believe that organic food is healthier are more likely to be willing to pay a premium for it.

- Perceptions of environmental impact: Consumers who believe that organic food is better for the environment are also more likely to be willing to pay a premium for it.

- Price: The price of organic food is often higher than the price of conventional food. Consumers who are willing to pay a premium for organic food are typically those who are more affluent.

- Availability: Organic food is not as widely available as conventional food. Consumers who are willing to pay a premium for organic food are typically those who live in areas where organic food is more readily available.

Research on willingness to pay for organic food

There have been a number of studies that have examined the willingness of consumers to pay for organic food. These studies have found that consumers are willing to pay a premium for organic food, but the amount of the premium varies depending on the factors mentioned above.

For example, one study found that consumers were willing to pay a premium of 20% for organic milk, but only a premium of 10% for organic eggs. The study also found that consumers were more willing to pay a premium for organic food if they believed that it was healthier and better for the environment.

Conclusion

The willingness of consumers to pay for organic food is a complex issue that is influenced by a variety of factors. Businesses that sell organic food need to understand these factors in order to price their products effectively.

Case Study7: The Government's Role in the Airline Industry

The airline industry is a heavily regulated industry, with the government playing a significant role in its operations. The government regulates the airline industry for a number of reasons, including:

- Safety: The government regulates the airline industry to ensure the safety of passengers and crew. This includes regulations on aircraft design, pilot training, and maintenance procedures.

- Competition: The government regulates the airline industry to ensure that there is fair competition between airlines. This includes regulations on pricing, routes, and mergers and acquisitions.

- Environmental protection: The government regulates the airline industry to protect the environment. This includes regulations on emissions and noise pollution.

The government's role in the airline industry is a complex issue with both benefits and drawbacks. The benefits of government regulation include:

- Increased safety: Government regulation has helped to improve the safety of air travel.

- Reduced pollution: Government regulation has helped to reduce the environmental impact of air travel.

- Fair competition: Government regulation has helped to ensure that there is fair competition between airlines.

The drawbacks of government regulation include:

- Increased costs: Government regulation can increase the costs of air travel for consumers.

- Less innovation: Government regulation can stifle innovation in the airline industry.

- Less choice: Government regulation can reduce the choices available to consumers.

The government's role in the airline industry is a controversial issue. There are strong arguments both for and against government regulation. Ultimately, the decision of whether or not to regulate the airline industry is a political one.

Here are some other examples of government interference in business:

- Antitrust laws: Antitrust laws are designed to prevent monopolies and protect competition. These laws can be used to break up monopolies or to prevent mergers that would reduce competition.

- Environmental regulations: Environmental regulations are designed to protect the environment. These regulations can affect businesses in a number of ways, such as by requiring them to reduce pollution or to use renewable energy sources.

- Labor regulations: Labor regulations are designed to protect workers' rights. These regulations can affect businesses in a number of ways, such as by requiring them to pay a minimum wage or to provide health insurance to their employees.

The extent of government interference in business varies from country to country. Some countries have a more laissez-faire approach, while others have a more interventionist approach. The decision of how much government interference is appropriate is a complex one that depends on a number of factors, such as the economic system, the political system, and the values of the society.

Case Study8: The Price Analysis of a New Product

A company is developing a new product and wants to conduct a price analysis to determine the best price to set. The company considers the following factors in its price analysis:

- The cost of production: The company needs to know how much it costs to produce the product in order to set a price that will cover its costs and make a profit.

- The competitive landscape: The company needs to know what other companies are charging for similar products in order to set a competitive price.

- The target market: The company needs to know what price its target market is willing to pay for the product in order to set a price that will be attractive to them.

- The company's goals: The company needs to consider its financial goals in setting a price. For example, if the company wants to quickly recoup its development costs, it may set a higher price.

The company uses a variety of methods to conduct its price analysis, including:

- Demand analysis: The company analyzes historical sales data to determine how demand for the product is likely to change with different prices.

- Cost-plus pricing: The company adds a markup to its cost of production to determine a price.

- Target costing: The company sets a target price and then works backward to determine the cost of production that is needed to achieve that price.

- Value-based pricing: The company determines the value that the product offers to customers and sets a price that reflects that value.

The company uses the results of its price analysis to set a price for the new product. The price is set to maximize the company's profits while also being attractive to its target market.

Here are some other factors that can be considered in price analysis:

- The product's features: Products with more features or benefits may be able to command a higher price.

- The product's quality: Products with higher quality may be able to command a higher price.

- The product's brand: Products with a strong brand may be able to command a higher price.

- The product's demand: Products with high demand may be able to command a higher price.

- The product's supply: Products with limited supply may be able to command a higher price.

Price analysis is an important tool for businesses to use in order to set prices that are both profitable and competitive. By considering a variety of factors, businesses can set prices that are likely to be successful in the marketplace.

www.ingramcontent.com/pod-product-compliance
Lightning Source LLC
LaVergne TN
LVHW070531070526
838199LV00075B/6757

9789356216129